KNOW
YOUR
BIBLE
SERIES

11

THE FOURTH GOSPEL
EPISTLES OF JOHN
REVELATION

ROY L. SMITH

ABINGDON PRESS
NASHVILLE

W9-BVK-972

The Fourth Gospel, Epistles of John, Revelation

No. 209226

Printed in U.S.A.

INTRODUCTION

Over the doorway of a certain church there hung a great sign whereon appeared an interesting legend:

WE TEACH THE BIBLE ONLY

Many people who passed that way gave mental approval to the sentiment on the assumption that it expressed a superior type of piety. There is something very praiseworthy about loyalty to the Christian Scriptures, and the present-day tide of interest in any study of the Holy Bible is to be commended by all means at our command. The weakness of the motto on the sign, however, lies in the fact that one cannot study the Bible without also studying other literature in order to know what the Bible really has to say for itself.

This principle is perfectly illustrated in the case of the New Testament books we are to investigate in this study. We shall discover as we proceed that if we were left dependent upon the scripture text alone, we should never really understand the deep meanings of some of the most significant passages.

In the first place, the Gospel of John makes use of several words which have been brought across from the writings of the ancient Greek philosophers. They are technical terms which had special meanings well understood by that generation, but which cannot be exactly translated into English.

We meet such a term in the very first verse of John's Gospel—namely, "the Word." This was a Greek word—*ho logos*—used to designate a well-known theological doctrine. It carried in its train a long succession of ideas, just as the modern word "evolution" suggests the whole philosophical system known as "Darwinism" to today's reader. The teacher who teaches "nothing but the Bible" cannot explain the meaning of the first verse of John's Gospel without going outside of the Bible for information concerning the exact meaning of "the Word."

Similarly in the case of the book of Revelation we are dealing with an elaborate system of symbols the exact meanings of which are not known to us. Rightly to interpret Revelation, it is necessary to go back into the literature of the century during which Revelation was written, and to discover, if possible, what the meaning of those symbols may have been when they were used in other writings.

It we found, for instance, that "horn" meant a certain idea in other books of the same time, we might assume that the word meant the same thing when used in John's book. And if "power" was symbolized by a certain figure in nonbiblical books of the same period, we could reasonably assume that the use of that symbol in Revelation meant "power."

These brief hints should suggest to the student that any sound interpretation of the elaborate symbolism of Revelation will depend upon help provided for us by the scholars who have worked their way with painstaking care through a mass of ancient writings. Here again, as in so many other instances, we find ourselves indebted to the scholars for our understandings of the Scriptures.

At least two of the books included in this study—the Fourth Gospel and Revelation—are so vast in their range of thought and so varied in their implications that it is impossible to do more than suggest their general nature and scope. The interested student is urged to consult a standard commentary for a more detailed exposition. We must be satisfied in this investigation to know the general message and purpose and to discover the social, political, and religious conditions which prevailed at the time the books were written.

Students desiring the assistance of a reliable commentary will find the one-volume *Abingdon Bible Commentary* among the most satisfactory and well within the price range desired by the average person. Those who are able to invest more liberally will do well to investigate *The Interpreter's Bible,* a comprehensive work in twelve volumes.

With the prayer that doors to new truth may here be opened for average students, this brief study is sent on its way.

Roy L. Smith

The John Books

1 What are the John Books?

Five books in the New Testament have long been associated with the name of the Apostle John. They are the Fourth Gospel, the book of Revelation, and three epistles—First, Second, and Third John. We shall study them as one group, although there are some valid objections to this plan.

2 What could those objections be?

Some might prefer to study the four Gospels together. They form a unit in the New Testament and have been circulated as such since the second century of the Christian Church. Such a study would be profitable, but the Fourth Gospel is so different from the other three that it can well be studied alone.

Others might prefer to study the Fourth Gospel alongside the letters of Paul, for their authors are the greatest minds whose writings appear in the New Testament. To compare them in the light of the times during which they were written would be a very interesting study in the development of Christian thought.

Then there are those who may object to including two books so different in outlook and purpose as the Fourth Gospel and Revelation in one study, in spite of the fact that both are linked with the name of John. This objection has good reason to support it, but the five books have been grouped together in this study for convenience' sake, and the contrasts between them will be pointed out as we proceed. At the very outset of our study, however, we are confronted with two of the most complex problems in all the New Testament.

3 What are those two problems?

The first is called the "Synoptic problem"; it cannot be investigated in detail until we come to Study No. 12 in this series. The other is called the "Johannine problem," and with it we shall deal at some length in this inquiry, though it is far too complex to allow us to give more than the most hurried explanation in the brief space at our disposal.

4 What is the Synoptic problem?

Even the most casual reader of the New Testament has noticed a certain duplication of material in the first three Gospels. Almost all of Mark is included in either Matthew or Luke, though both these books contain much additional material. Then they have other material in common beside the Marcan passages, and each has some that is peculiar to itself.

The thoughtful student, faced with these variations and similarities, immediately begins to ask questions. Why are there these differences? Which Gospel gives the original and correct report? Certainly, as in the case of the Lord's Prayer, both versions cannot be verbatim reports (Matthew 6:9b-13; Luke 11:24). These similarities and differences in the three Gospels, with all the questions that they raise, make up the "Synoptic problem," and that will constitute a part of Study No. 12.

5 What is the Johannine problem?

That which is known to scholars as the Johannine problem is an equally long list of questions concerning the authorship, purposes, theology, and Christian concepts of the various books associated with the name of John. To this we now proceed, beginning our study with an inquiry concerning the Fourth Gospel.

6 What is the Fourth Gospel?

It is, by common agreement, the most important of the John books and, judged by almost any standard, the most important writing of the New Testament. Its author, whoever he may have been, was a thinker of the first rank. It can hardly be disputed that the Fourth Gospel has had the greatest influence on the development and direction of Christianity of any single book in the New Testament.

7 When was the book written?

By common agreement among scholars of all shades of opinion it is conceded to have been one of the last books of the New Testament to take form. In fixing the exact date of its composition, however, we are confronted with many difficulties. First of all, the book itself makes no statement in the matter.

There are indications that it was known among the Church Fathers as early as A.D. 130, and to get such a book into circulation and into the thinking of the Church would have required several years. It must therefore have been written sometime earlier. On the other hand, there is good reason for believing that the Gospel of Luke was written about A.D. 90, and there is distinct evidence that the author of the Fourth Gospel was familiar with that work. He could hardly have made such an acquaintance until at least a few years after its composition. By this process of reasoning the majority of scholars believe the Fourth Gospel must have been written sometime between A.D. 95 and A.D. 115, or at least seventy-five years following the crucifixion of Jesus. It can be said to represent the convictions of a great Christian scholar of about A.D. 100.

8 What was the status of Christianity in A.D. 100?

Christianity had broken completely with Judaism and was setting out to conquer the world as an independent movement. It proposed to make converts among all peoples (John 3:16). So strongly did it appeal to the Greek mind that at least small congregations of Christians were to be found in every city of importance in the East. It was, however, facing at least four serious dangers—the opposition of the Jews, the enmity of the Roman Empire, the rivalry of the followers of John the Baptist, and certain heresies which were growing up inside the Christian movement. In addition, it was beset by certain inevitable difficulties inherent in the movement itself.

9 What were the most crucial of those problems?

No two congregations faced exactly the same problems, some being acute in one community and others more threatening in other communities. In general, however, it may be said that there were eight major facts with which the Church had to deal: (1) the stubborn opposition of the Jews, (2) the open opposition of the Roman Empire, (3) the rival claims of the followers of John the Baptist, (4) the heresies within the Christian movement, (5) the necessity of translating Christian thought into a Greek vocabulary, (6) the failing hope of the Christians because of the delay in Jesus' second coming, (7) the lack of a formal statement of the Christian position capable of satisfying the demands of the Greek mind, (8) the absence of uniform organization of the Church itself.

10 Why were the Jews opposed to the Christians?

In A.D. 70 the Roman general Titus destroyed the city of Jerusalem in putting down a rebellion. As a result the national life of the Jews, centering in the Temple, came to an end and the Jewish people everywhere in the empire were under suspicion. Partly as a result of the destruction of Jerusalem, and partly as a result of the exclusive spirit of the mother church there, the Christian movement died out among the Jews and became almost exclusively Gentile. By the year 100 practically all ties were cut and the Gentile congregations were on their own. They had not, however, developed any great leadership capable of commanding the support of the entire Church, and the individual congregations were pretty largely left to themselves.

The Jews, on the other hand, had been zealous missionaries of their faith for many years and had been able to attract considerable numbers of Greek who were unsatisfied with the barren philosophies common among their thinkers. The Jewish synagogues were filled with converts from the Gentile world, and to these the young Christian Church made a definite appeal. The Jews, therefore, found themselves pitted against the pagans and the Christians, and their conflict with the latter was made the more bitter because of the Christian preaching that the Jews were, themselves, apostate. Concerning this we shall make further inquiry when we study the controversies of the Fourth Gospel (Question 74).

11 Why was the Roman Empire opposed to the Christians?

For the purpose of conserving the peace of the realm the Roman government assumed the right to supervise all religious movements, and any suspected of "subversive tendencies" were put under the ban. At first Christianity was regarded as a Jewish sect and as such enjoyed immunity, for Judaism was one of the tolerated religions of the empire. For a time Christian leaders took advantage of this status and avoided conflicts with the Roman authorities. In time, however the empire recognized the basic differences between the two, partly because of their own antagonisms, and the persecutions began. Of this we shall make further inquiry in connection with our study of the book of Revelation.

12 **What part did the followers of John the Baptist play?**

Christian generally have been inclined to overlook the great ministry of John the Baptist among the Jews prior to the time that Jesus launched his career, but it seems certain that in that generation the Baptist got more attention than Jesus did. His preaching seems to have attracted vast multitudes, and we know that he gave the authorities great concern. Long after his death congregations of his followers were found by Christian missionaries scattered throughout Asia Minor (Acts 18:25; 19:3-4). The evidence in the Fourth Gospel indicates that there was a strong following of the prophet in Ephesus which believed that John, not Jesus, was the long-looked for Jewish Messiah. These had to be converted or absorbed by the Christian movement if the Johnite sect was not to become another rival of Christianity.

13 **What were the heresies inside the Christian movement?**

They were as varied as today's cults and sects, but because of the lack of exact historical data it is difficult to describe them in detail. The Greeks were much given to speculative thought, and the half-formulated Christian position left room for vagaries of all kinds. There was no one in the Christian movement, however, who had the authority to brand the heretics as being heretical and to forbid them the use of the name "Christian." Any heresy that attached itself to the Christian movement could claim it was authentic and become just one more obstacle to impede the progress of the movement. When we study the First Epistle of John we shall learn more about this matter, as also in our study of Revelation. Likewise, as our study of the Fourth Gospel proceeds, we shall come upon this problem frequently.

14 **What about the Greek vocabulary?**

In spite of its independence of Judaism, Christianity still preached its gospel in terms of Jewish theology, Jewish Scriptures, and Jewish thought forms. The three Gospels which preceded John's Gospel presented Jesus as a Jewish Messiah who had been foretold by Hebrew prophets. The great missionaries of the Christian movement had been Jews who had broken with organized Judaism for Christ's sake, and their terminology was all Jewish. This meant that it was necessary not only to convert people to faith in Jesus but also to explain Jewish terms to them before they could understand the message.

15 What did the Second Coming have to do with the case?

The hope of an early return of Jesus was one of the conspicuous doctrines of the Christians. It was agreed by all that he had not performed the work of a Messiah during his lifetime, and a second appearance was necessary if such an expectation was to be fulfilled. Paul had promised such a second coming, and the hope of that promise had sustained the Christians through many discouragements. As the years passed and there was no visible indication of any such immediate return, widespread skepticism developed and even the stout-hearted became discouraged. Something was needed to counteract this attitude of defeatism.

16 Why was there no formal statement of belief?

When the Christians first rushed out of Galilee with the thrilling news that Jesus ws risen from the dead, they went everywhere preaching, "He has risen!" This was their first great doctrine. When men accepted this as being true, they were asked to make just one simple affirmation—"Jesus is Lord" (Romans 10:9; I Corinthians 12:3; Philippians 2:11). By the year 100, however, the primitive age of the church was over, and few if any remained alive who had seen or heard Jesus in person. Whatever knowledge the Christians had of his life or teachings was secondhand, in the form of either literature or tradition. Christians who had never heard Jesus had to formulate beliefs concerning him on the basis of this hearsay evidence. Had the Church been thoroughly organized, this might have been a comparatively simple matter. Accredited scholars could have been assigned the task of preparing a statement of Christian doctrine, and all men could have been asked to subscribe to that standard. But there was no such world-wide authority, and the

Christian movement suffered as the result of a perversion of a great doctrine.

17 What was the perverted doctrine?

Christianity was a religion of the spirit. It taught the profound truth that everyone who had faith in Jesus Christ was, as a consequence, in touch with the Holy Spirit of the living God. Accordingly it seemed that all Christians stood on the same level; the humblest believer had the same right to interpret Christian facts as had the most famous missionary or the most learned scholar, and some of them availed themselves of the privilege. The result was great confusion, even the most absurd teachings claiming the authority of the "Spirit" for their absurdity. The resulting heresies became serious threats to the movement.

18 Why was the Church not unified?

It lacked two essentials of unity: (1) it lacked any standard interpretation of Jesus adapted to the Greek mind with which it had to work, and (2) each local congregation—and individual—was independent of all the rest and a law unto itself.

19 What did John's Gospel have to do with all this?

The Gospel of John was an effort to interpret the Christian faith to the Greek mind, and to provide a statement concerning the work and person of Jesus which would convince pagans and Christians alike that a new life principle had entered the world when Jesus made his appearance among men.

20 Who wrote the Gospel of John?

This question plunges us at once into the heart of the Johannine problem, and the most honest answer is that *no one knows*. There are numerous beliefs concerning the matter, but none are capable of complete proof. Reputable scholars are extremely cautious about making sweeping statements.

21 What does the Gospel itself say?

The reader will note that, so far as the Fourth Gospel itself is concerned, it is anonymous. There is no verse in the book that names the author, and no hint except in one vague verse.

22 What is that vague verse?

John 21:24 says, "This is the disciple who . . . has written these things; and we know that his testimony is true."

23 What does this mean?

Scholars are almost unanimous in the belief that the original composition ended with the twentieth chapter. Certainly the last verses of that chapter form a definite conclusion—*"Now Jesus did many other signs . . . which are not written in this book; but these are written that you may believe that Jesus is the Christ, the Son of God, and that believing you may have life in his name."* The meaning of these words is very plain; the entire book was written for the purpose of proving that Jesus was the Christ, the Son of God, and of persuading people to believe in him as such. The proofs offered included a series of "signs" which had been chosen out of many which might have been recorded.

Sometime afterward some unknown person (the scholars call him a "redactor") felt it would strengthen the Gospel's argument if its authenticity was guaranteed, and to offer such authentication the twenty-first chapter was added. This chapter states very frankly that "the beloved disciple" was the author.

24 Was this not a strange thing to do?

Not at all. We must remember that at that time the book was not esteemed to be "scripture," but a purely private writing produced by someone well known to the Christians, and with which any individual might do as he pleased. But the "redactor" really thought he was adding to the merits of the book by vouching for it, as in the case of a modern book which carries an "introduction" by some friend of the author as an assurance to the public that the things the author says may be accepted as reliable.

25 Who was the beloved disciple?

Again we have to say we do not know. The person who wrote the twenty-first chapter of John knew who he was, and the first readers of the Gospel must have known who he was. But nowhere is he named, and we have to study the matter with care. Even then there is much division of opinion on the subject.

There have been at least three theories in the matter.

26 **What are those three theories?**

1. That he was John the disciple, the son of Zebedee.
2. That he was John the elder (or presbyter) of Ephesus.
3. That he was an unknown young man of Jerusalem. Then there are those who think the "unknown young man" may have become John the elder in later years.

27 **What does the Fourth Gospel say about the beloved disciple?**

The last chapter of John's Gospel tells a story of an appearance of Jesus to a company of disciples at the "Sea of Tiberias" (21:1). Among them was one "whom Jesus loved" (21:7, 20). In telling of the appearance a conversation between Jesus and Peter is reported in which Jesus said something about "the beloved disciple" which had left the impression among the Christians that he would not die (21:23). We gather from the chapter that he had died, however, and that the writer of the chapter felt it necessary to clear up the misunderstanding of what Jesus had actually said. In doing so he makes the flat statement that "the beloved disciple" wrote the Gospel of John (21:24).

28 **Could the son of Zebedee have been "the beloved disciple"?**

It is probably true that the average Christian so believes, but that may be because he has never studied the question carefully. Before we decide the matter it is necessary to consider certain facts in the case:

1. The few references we have to John the son of Zebedee in the Gospels do not seem to support the theory that he was Jesus' favorite. It is true that he was one of the three who shared Jesus' inner confidences on several special occasions, but in each of these cases Peter, not John, is named first. This seems to indicate that Peter might have been Jesus' favorite (Matthew 17:1; Mark 9:2; Luke 9:28; also Matthew 26:37 and Mark 14:33).

2. In Mark 10:35-37 he is represented as one who sought special privileges and is called a "son of thunder" (Mark 3:17), which suggests an aggressive, noisy, blatant sort of person.

This impression is supported by Luke's testimony (9:51-56), which portrays him as a vindictive, hot-headed, impulsive individual. Mark also hints that he was inclined to be jealous and assertive (9:38), one whom Jesus had to curb.

3. It is known that he was a Galilean fisherman (Mark 1:19). Greek was spoken in Galilee in a limited fashion, but the Fourth Gospel is written in an excellent style which one would hardly expect from a Galilean fisherman.

4. The Fourth Gospel makes use of Greek ideas which were produced by Greek philosophers, and though a Galilean fisherman might make himself familiar with such in his mature years, it is not exactly what one would expect. Certainly one would not expect such a one as John the son of Zebedee to handle profound philosophical terms and ideas as the author of the Fourth Gospel does.

These facts would argue against the fisherman's authorship, but they by no means make it impossible.

29 Do we have any other evidence?

There is evidence outside the New Testament both for and against the theory of the fisherman's authorship.

How the name of John came to be associated with the Gospel no one knows, but from the time of Irenaeus (*ca.* A.D. 180) until perhaps a century ago, it was commonly believed that John, the son of Zebedee and one of the original disciples of Jesus, was the author. A small sect known as the "Alogi" (rejectors of the Logos) raised some questions during the second century but were given scant consideration. There has never been a New Testament in which the Gospel has not been associated with the name of John, but the name has long been a common one among all people and our problem is to determine *which John* wrote the book. In doing so we become dependent upon the traditions and the writings of the early Church Fathers.

30 What do the traditions say?

For many years it was believed that John the son of Zebedee migrated to Ephesus sometime before the destruction of Jerusalem (A.D. 70). If he had been a youth of sixteen or thereabouts when he joined Jesus' band of disciples, this tradition might easily have been true, and he might have lived

14

to an advanced age and have written the Gospel in A.D. 95-100. But this tradition must be tested alongside the testimony of the Church Fathers.

31 What do they have to say?

There are four witnesses: Irenaeus, who wrote about A.D. 180; Polycrates, who wrote about the same time; Papias, who wrote about A.D. 140; and a fourth, who wrote about A.D. 116.

Irenaeus says he was in his youth a pupil of Polycarp, the bishop of Smyrna. That great Christian had taught him Christian doctrines which he, in turn, had learned from the Apostle John. Since Ephesus and Smyrna are not far apart, this testimony lends credibility to the idea that John spent some years in Ephesus.

Polycrates, the bishop of Ephesus, addressed a letter to the bishop of Rome about the same time, in which he says that Ephesus had been the home of John "who reclined on the bosom of the Lord." This would be extremely valuable evidence if we were sure that Zebedee's son "reclined." That, however, is not proved.

About A.D. 140 a Christian named Papias wrote some historical papers. None of his writings are now in existence, but Eusebius, the great church historian of the early fourth century, has preserved several quotations, one of which makes it perfectly plain that in A.D. 140 two Johns were associated with the church at Ephesus—one dead and the other living, both of whom had been known as "disciples." In another quotation Papias says that both James and John died as martyrs, and in the case of James we know from other evidence that Papias' statement is true (Acts 12:2). Whether he is equally correct in the case of John, we do not know.

Doubt concerning the Apostle's residence in Ephesus is raised by the fact that a series of seven letters was written by a Church Father in A.D. 116, one of which was addressed to the church at Ephesus. In it the Ephesians are congratulated on their association with Paul, but no mention is made of John, and surely, if the Apostle had lived in Ephesus as late as A.D. 95, he would have been the most famous and conspicuous Christian in the world and one who could not have been overlooked. This proves nothing, of course, beyond the fact that there is some reason for doubting that the Apostle lived in Ephesus for any length of time, or during the late years of his life.

32 What do we know definitely about John's last days?

We know he was still alive in A.D. 48, for Paul refers to him in his letter to the Galatian churches (Galatians 2:9). Jesus predicted that James and John would suffer martyrdom (Mark 10:39), and various ancient writings, including Papias' famous quotation, refer to their death. All this seems to show that the Apostle died many years before the Fourth Gospel as written, but the case is not proved.

33 What can we believe about the apostolic authorship?

There are five reasons for questioning it, although none is conclusive: (1) the Gospel itself makes no such claim; (2) the tradition that he was martyred cannot be set aside lightly; (3) there is no contemporary evidence to prove or disprove his authorship, and the first actual reference to the Gospel in which the name of John is used occurs in the writings of Theophilus of Antioch, who wrote in A.D. 181 and called the book "The Gospel of John"; (4) it is unlikely that a Galilean fisherman could have become so skilled in philosophy and classic Greek as to produce a writing so profound; (5) the appended twenty-first chapter says that "the beloved disciple" was the author, and this appelation does not seem to fit any description we have of John the son of Zebedee.

34 What do we know about "the beloved disciple"?

He is mentioned five times in the Fourth Gospel (13:23; 19:26; 20:2; 21:7, 20). In John 21:2 five of the original band of disciples are named as being among those at the seashore, but it is also stated that "two others of his disciples" were also there—which is proof that the word "disciple" was sometimes applied to others than those of the original twelve. The "disciple whom Jesus loved" might have been one of the twelve, or he might have been an outsider.

In the scene about the table on the occasion of the last supper, according to the Fourth Gospel, it is reported that "one of his disciples, whom Jesus loved, was lying close to the breast of Jesus" (13:23). Nowhere is it said that Jesus was with the twelve *alone.* Mark reports Jesus' reply to a question in which he said that the betrayer was to come from among the twelve (Mark 14:20), as if others might have been present at the supper. Some excellent scholars deduce from this that some genteel youth from Jerusalem, perhaps in his early teens, was present at the supper and was known to the others as "the disciple whom Jesus loved."

35 Who could he have been?

No one attempts to say precisely, but attention is called to the fact that when Jesus commends his mother to "the beloved disciple" (John 19:26) he takes her to his home "from that hour." John the son of Zebedee had no other home than the one in Galilee, so far as we know, and he could hardly have escorted Mary there "from that hour." If the "beloved disciple" had been a youth from Jerusalem, it would have been perfectly natural for Jesus to have asked him to care for his mother, and for him to have taken her back to the city and kept her in his home until after the Sabbath was over. It would, furthermore, have been natural for him to accompany Peter to the tomb on the morning of the Resurrection (John 20:3) in order to get news for Mary, and equally natural for him, a vigorous youth, to have outrun the aging disciple (20:4).

From the foregoing it is not impossible to assume that Jesus had won the love of a personable and winsome youth of Jerusalem, and that the boy had attached himself to the company of disciples, being affectionately known as "the disciple whom Jesus loved." Because of the Master's fondness for him he became a member of the band during those last days and shared those associations. As such he could easily have been a member of the company at the lake (21:2) and been one of "two others of his disciples." Just at this point Papias throws a little light on the problem.

36 What does Papias have to say?

We have already noted the fact that Papias mentions two Johns—one living and the other dead—known as "disciples" and associated with the church at Ephesus. Many years afterward two tombs of "John" were shown at Ephesus. Papias wrote as though John the Apostle was dead and as though John "the presbyter" (sometimes called "elder"), whom he had

17

heard in his youth, was another person. It is an established fact that there was a Christian preacher in Ephesus of considerable fame known as "John the Elder" about the year A.D. 100 (II John 1; III John 1), and it would have been easy to confuse his name with that of John the Apostle and the son of Zebedee. The "beloved disciple" was well known to the Church in A.D. 100, so well known indeed that it was not necessary to mention his name (21:24).

37 What about "John the Elder" and the Fourth Gospel?

From sources entirely outside the New Testament we have word of a highly honored preacher in Ephesus known as "John the Elder." There are those who believe that he was the youth of Jerusalem grown older and now a leader of the Church.

38 What can we conclude about the matter?

It is impossible to be positive about too much in such a case. There were two or three Johns: John the Apostle, John the Elder, and "the beloved disciple," who may also have been named John—who may even have become John the Elder. Because of the impossibility of determining exactly who the author was, we shall be content from this point on to refer to him simply as "John."

39 Where was the Gospel written?

The very earliest Christian tradition ascribes the Fourth Gospel to the Ephesian church. There may be wide differences of opinion concerning the identity of the author, but there is no difference concerning the fact that the Gospel is the product of *someone at Ephesus*. It seems to be agreed by all that it was written by "the John who was the head of the church at Ephesus."

40 What kind of city was Ephesus?

There is a sense in which it could have been called the capital of the Eastern world. In reality it consisted of two cities—one, a commercial center, was built around the harbor; and the other, a religious and cultural center, was built around the famous temple of Artemis ("Diana" in Latin—Acts 19:23-41) about a mile away. Through it flowed tides of travel and commerce as well as of Greek thought and culture. According to tradition it was the birthplace of Homer, and according to fact it was the home of several vigorous intellectual movements. Greek philosophers found a congenial atmosphere there and flourished in a manner that rivaled Athens itself. It impressed Paul as being a city which offered unusual evangelistic opportunities (I Corinthians 16:9), and to it and the church there he gave his best ministry through several years. In time it came to have a unique importance in the Christian movement.

41 **How was Ephesus related to the Christian movement?**

Until the destruction of Jerusalem (A.D. 70) the church in that city was the center of the Christian enterprise. The presence of the apostles, the historical associations, the sentimental connections, and the priority of organization gave it an authority which was respected everywhere. It will be remembered that Paul came to Jerusalem to secure approval of his mission to the Gentiles, and delicate matters of doctrine and discipline were usually referred to the elders there for decision. This was always a matter of courtesy, of course, for they had no legal authority of any kind which empowered them to discipline either churches or individuals.

With the razing of Jerusalem the Christians were left without leadership for a time, and the church at Ephesus gradually forged ahead and became Jerusalem's successor. By the close of the first century it had become the spearhead of the Christian movement. Some really remarkable achievements must be credited to the Ephesian congregation, among them being the honor of having made the first collection of Paul's letters, which, in time, became the forerunner of the New Testament. In many ways the Ephesian church set the standards for the Christians of all the world, and in a very real sense it can be said that Ephesus was the intellectual and ecclesiastical center of the Christian world for many years.

42 **Why did the Ephesian church prosper?**

One of the chief reasons seems to have been the fact that it had exceptional leadership. It is known that Paul gave to it his longest ministry (Acts 19:8-20:1; 20:17-38) and left there a heroic and thriving congregation. Then whoever the author of the

19

Fourth Gospel may have been, we know he was a thinker of the first rank and a spiritual leader without a peer. He must have been an inspiring pastor for a group of Christians just beginning their Christian experience. It could hardly have been possible for a people to have had the benefit of so great a pastor without themselves becoming great in the process of listening to him. Yet withal it was no small matter to launch a new religion in such a city as Ephesus.

43 What was the special hazard of Ephesus?

Because of the cosmopolitan culture of the city and the variety of Greek thought to be encountered in its lecture halls, a new faith which hoped to survive in Ephesus had to be prepared to stand up against the best minds in Asia. Paul anticipated many difficulties there and solemnly warned the elders of the Church to be on their guard against heresies (Acts 20:29). According to the best evidence we have, it was in Ephesus that the Gnostic heresy made its first appearance. The pride of the Ephesians in their famous goddess. Artemis and the wide range of religious thought that was current in the city created an atmosphere that was both an advantage and a danger.

44 How is all this known?

The information has come down to us by two routes: (1) by tradition, and (2) by paragraphs embedded here and there in the writings of the Church Fathers. Moreover, the Fourth Gospel fits into exactly such a setting, and when we understand that scene we understand the Gospel.

45 For what purpose was the Fourth Gospel written?

The author makes the purpose of his book perfectly clear in the last verse of his writing. *"These are written,"* he says, *"that you may believe that Jesus is the Christ, the Son of God, and that believing you may have life in his name"* (20:31). This means that his was a double purpose—(1) that men might be convinced that Jesus was the Son of God, and (2) that, being convinced, they might receive the benefits he had to confer.

46 How did he proceed?

Certain materials lay ready at hand. First, there was a great body of oral tradition current among the Christians—stories about Jesus, sayings of his which were quoted somewhat as sayings of Washington and Lincoln are quoted among the American people, teachings of his which had been passed down from father to son. Christianity had now reached the third generation of believers.

In the second place, there were three Gospels current among the Christians, and these were being read alongside the letters of Paul in many Christian congregations, keeping the Gospel story alive among the people. These had the effect of educating the people concerning the teachings of Jesus, his activities while alive among men, and the major meanings of his ministry.

To John, however, it appeared perfectly plain that some valid explanation of this amazing person, Jesus of Nazareth, must be offered to the thoughtful Greeks. Certainly he had been no ordinary person. Indeed, no man had ever lived like him, talked like him, or taught as he had taught. But even more, through believing in his name John had himself come into a transforming personal spiritual experience which he could explain in only one way—Jesus was the Son of God and had imparted to him the gift of eternal life. All this he undertook to explain to his generation in terms they could understand, for the purpose of converting them to his viewpoint, of persuading them also to "believe in his name" so that they, too, might receive the gift of life. In preparing his explanation John wrote the Fourth Gospel, and in writing he followed a perfectly clear program. That program produced a book of peculiar literary style, entirely different from anything else in the New Testament.

47 What was his program?

We must keep clearly in mind from the outset one central fact. *John believed that Jesus was God become flesh.* His book sets out to prove that, and every detail in it is shaped to that end. As we study it with care we discover four very significant things about it.

48 What is the first thing we discover?

It is very evident from the start that John is not writing a biography of Jesus nor a history of his work. Rather, he is writing an argument which he believes will prove that Jesus was the Son of God. In doing so he makes no pretense of giving all

21

the facts concerning Jesus' life with which he is familiar, but he offers only those which will support his position.

49 What is the second thing we discover?

He is addressing his appeal to the best Greek minds and, as a consequence, makes use of terms familiar to them. In some cases he gives these terms new meanings, and in other cases he adapts them to his purpose. But it is very evident that he is transplanting the whole Christian doctrine from one cultural soil to another—from the Jewish to the Greek.

50 What is the third thing we discover?

In making his appeal to the learned Greeks of his time he has to meet certain objections, with the result that his book includes a series of controversies.

51 What is the fourth thing we discover?

In making his argument in behalf of Jesus' divinity John produced a book which differs very widely from the Synoptics, so much so that they represent two entirely different approaches to the problem of Jesus.

52 How does John's book differ from the Synoptics?

The difference is due to a radical difference in objectives. Luke, for instance, says that his book was written for the express purpose of setting down "in order" the whole story of Jesus (Luke 1:3), whereas John says he has presented an argument designed to convince his readers that Jesus was the Son of God (John 20:31). The changed conditions of the times required that the presentation of the Christian cause should follow a new line.

53 How had the times changed?

During those first years following the Resurrection the Christian preachers went everywhere telling the amazing story of Jesus. The world had been made more or less familiar with that report, and men were asking, "What kind of a man was this Jesus?" The thoughtful Greek was asking for an explanation, and this explanation John undertook to give. He confessed very frankly that he was not attempting to duplicate the work already done by the three Gospels, but said that he had selected the facts which would prove his contention—that Jesus was God made flesh. The first generation had asked, "Who is this man Jesus?" and the third generation, for whom John wrote, asked, "What was Jesus?"

54 What difference did the change make?

A careful study of John's Gospel shows at least three distinct differences in his presentation:

1. In the course of almost a hundred years the Christian message had unfolded and grown. The Christian experiences of a century had thrown new light upon it, just as a lifetime of devout living throws light upon an early conversion. The three Gospels represent the observations men had made of the early life of Jesus. The Fourth Gospel represents the conclusions the Church had reached concerning that life after many years of Christian experience.

2. During the course of a hundred years political changes had taken place which altered the whole course of the Christian movement. The Jewish national life had been crushed with the destruction of Jerusalem; Christianity had broken loose from Judaism; and the movement had risen from the lowly status of a Jewish sect to that dignified position of being a world religion bidding for world acceptance. In the process of moving over from its Jewish cradle to its universal home Christianity itself had changed very materially. This called for a complete restatement of the Christian faith.

3. Separated by a century from the living presence of Jesus, Christianity was in danger of becoming a mere tradition, in which a glorious life would be venerated. John himself had had a great inner experience. He had felt a new "life" coming in upon him as a consequence of his "belief on the name of Jesus." He was sure that Jesus, risen and alive, was eager to establish and maintain personal fellowship with all men (3:16), and he wrote for the purpose of persuading men to "believe" in order that they might experience that fellowship. This was an effort to transfer Christianity, making it a religion of experience instead of a religion of historical tradition.

55 How does all this appear in John's Gospel?

If the student will keep in mind the unique position John

occupies in the New Testament, he will see the significance of at least twelve facts which stand out in a comparison of his Gospel with the Synoptics.

56   What is the first fact?

It seems quite evident that John is familiar with the work of Mark and Luke (compare John 6:7 with Mark 6:37, John 12:3, 5 with Mark 14:3, 5, John 14:31 with Mark 14:42, John 18:18 with Mark 14:54, John 18:39 with Mark 15:9, John 5:8-9 with Mark 2:11-12). In his story of Martha and Mary (12:1-8) he seems to have combined elements of Mark's (14:3-9) and Luke's (7:36-50) accounts. He agrees with Luke in saying that Pilate scourged Jesus in the hope that the Jews might be dissuaded from demanding the death penalty (compare John 19:1 with Luke 23:22). Even more important is the fact that John and Luke report the first Resurrection appearance as having occurred in Jerusalem, whereas Mark and Matthew assign it to Galilee. In contrast to his use of Mark and Luke it is noticeable that John ignores Matthew entirely.

57   What is the second fact?

John seems to have an exact mind, for he gives names, dates, places, etc., with a strict regard for accuracy. The Synoptics say, for instance, that Jesus was crucified on the day following the Passover meal (Mark 14:12; 15:1; Matthew 26:1-2; 27:1; Luke 22:1, 7), while John says it was the day on the afternoon of which the Pascal lambs were slaughtered that they might be eaten the same evening after sunset (John 19:14, 31, 42). In other words, though all agree that it was on Friday, the Synoptics date it on Nisan 15 while John fixes it on the date Nisan 14. Since secular business would not have been transacted during the hours of the Passover festival, scholars are strongly of the opinion that John's report is the correct one. It is interesting also to note that John identifies Annas, the ex-high priest, as the villain in the plot (18:13)—which is undoubtedly true. The Jews regarded him as the true high priest, though Caiaphas, his son-in-law, occupied the post by Roman appointment.

58   What is the third fact?

He was more interested in theology than in history. He did

not set out to compile a "life" of Jesus, but to interpret him. This is apparent in his rearrangement of the material. Whereas the Synoptics report the cleansing of the Temple as one of the last of Jesus' acts, John reports it very early in his story (compare John 2:13 ff. with Matthew 21:12 ff.; Mark 11:15 ff.; Luke 19:45 ff.). The reason for this difference seems to be the difference in their purposes. The Synoptics were concerned with chronology, and John was concerned with significance. John wanted to establish Jesus' divine authority at the outset.

59 What is the fourth fact?

The Synoptic authors all speak of Jesus' habit of teaching in parables, whereas if the Fourth Gospel were the only one we would have no way of knowing that Jesus ever used parables at all. On the other hand, John seems to have had a special interest of his own—an interest in Jesus' miracles.

60 What is the fifth fact?

It is the difference between John and the Synoptics in their treatment of the meaning of miracles. The Synoptics tell of the cures of demoniacs, but John mentions none of these. On the other hand, he tells the story of Jesus' authority over nature—of changing water into wine (2:1 ff.), multiplying loaves (6:1 ff), walking on the sea (6:16 ff.). Whereas the Synoptics report the miracles as evidences of Jesus' compassion, John reports them as proof of his divinity (compare Mark 1:41 and 8:2 with John 2:11). In the Synoptics, Jesus is reported as demanding faith as a condition upon which he would perform miracles (Mark 6:5-6), but in the Fourth Gospel his healings and other miracles are offered as a reason why men should have faith in him (2:11; 4:53-54; 6:2, 14; 7:31; 9:16; 11:45).

In his argument to prove the divinity of Jesus, John makes use of seven "signs" which he has chosen out of a long list which he might have cited. The number seven symbolized completeness to the Oriental mind, and in citing seven signs John assumed he was offering a *complete* proof of Jesus' divine powers (2:1-11; 4:46-54; 5:1-18; 6:1-15; 6:16-21; 9:1-41; 11:1-46).

61 What is the sixth fact?

There is a marked contrast between the teachings of the

Synoptics and the teachings of the Fourth Gospel. In the first three Gospels, Jesus deals with great moral issues of everyday life, giving particular emphasis to the Kingdom of God and how to enter it. By means of parables and short pithy sentences which state principles they set forth the fundamental ideas, and only rarely do we come upon a long discourse on an abstract theme. The Sermon on the Mount, for instance, is a collection of sayings dealing with a wide variety of themes. In the Synoptics, Jesus talks very little about himself and seldom discusses his peculiar relationship to God.

The Fourth Gospel proceeds from an entirely different point of view. Its discourses are long discussions of abstract themes bearing on such subjects as Jesus' own nature, his divinity, his relationship to God, the nature and efficacy of faith, etc. Whereas the Synoptics think of faith as an act of trusting God, John thinks of it as a matter of believing in Jesus' divinity. The three Gospels put the emphasis on a moral act, and the Fourth puts it on the theological correctness of the act.

62 What is the seventh fact?

There is a considerable difference in the two accounts of Jesus' ministry. From the Synoptics one gets the impression that it lasted only about a year, whereas John represents it as covering at least three annual feasts (2:13; 7:14; 11:55). If we had no other record than Mark's, we would not know that Jesus did any preaching until after the Baptist's imprisonment (Mark 1:14), but John tells us that the two preached for a while at least at the same time (3:23). The Synoptics describe Jesus' ministry as though it had occurred almost entirely in Galilee, and, except for a few trips outside that province (Mark 7:24; 8:27; 10:1), no mention is made of any trip to Jerusalem until the fatal journey that led up to his crucifixion. John, on the other hand, lays the scene of Jesus' ministry in Jerusalem and represents his visits to Galilee almost as side excursions (John 2:1 ff.; 4:43 ff.; 7:1 ff.). He seems to be thinking of Jesus as one who laid siege to Judaism in its own stronghold.

63 What is the eighth fact?

There is a marked difference between the two portraits of Jesus. The Synoptics tell many incidents which describe his humanity, and John seems almost deliberately to suppress such stories. He never hints that Jesus was in any way subject to temptation, nor that he was ever in desperate need. No mention is made of his agonized prayer in the Garden, of his desperate cry from the cross, or of the temptations that followed his baptism. He is represented as having divine insight (1:42, 48; 2:24; 4:16; 5:6; 6:61, 64; 13:18; 16:19) and as being the master of the forces that play upon his life (7:30; 8:20, 59: 9:11; 10:39; 12:36; 18:6; also 2:4; 7:10; 12:16; 13:27). The Synoptics portray a man, and John portrays the Son of God.

64 What is the ninth fact?

There is a marked difference in the role the two accounts assign to Jesus. The Synoptics undertake to prove that Jesus was the long-looked-for Jewish Messiah. In a variety of ways they try to fit him into the picture the prophets have drawn of "the anointed one." John, on the other hand, presents him as "the Logos," or the incarnation of God, and gives scant attention to his messianic aspects. This difference is further explained by the tenth fact.

65 What is the tenth fact?

The Synoptics are all phrased in Jewish terms, as though they were attempting to convince Jews. John, on the other hand, borrows many Greek philosophic terms (Word, light, life, etc.), as if he were trying to interpret Jesus to the Greek mind. Scholars are not agreed as to whether or not John was trained in Greek philosophy, but they are agreed that he appropriated many Greek terms and adapted them to his message, somewhat as an Oriental might make use of popular terms in modern American speech even before he was fully aware of all their significance.

66 What is the eleventh fact?

Matthew and Luke tell beautiful stories of a miraculous birth and a physical and intellectual development on the part of Jesus (Luke 2:52). John ignores all such; he presents him as the incarnation of God—as one who had existed long before his birth and who burst upon the world as an astounding, full-orbed revelation of God. In the Synoptics, Jesus moves from one position to another; he alters his plans and techniques as if

27

he might be experimenting with his procedure; he grows in effectiveness and knowledge. John represents him as the perfect God-man who needs no such development.

67 What is the twelfth fact?

In most instances in the Synoptics, Jesus seems reluctant to claim his messiahship or allow it to be claimed for him. He cautions people against telling of their cures or the exercise of his amazing powers. In John he seems anxious to assert his supernatural status from the start and boldly proclaims his divinity.

68 What do all these facts means?

They mean that John undertook deliberately to set Jesus forth in an entirely new light—a light that had dawned upon the Church since the time the Synoptics were written and which reflects the spiritual experience through which the Church (and John as an individual) had passed. The Fourth Gospel contains the conclusions of a great spiritual genius, about A.D. 100, concerning Jesus—conclusions which involved him in at least three major controversies.

69 What were those controversies?

1. The controversy with the followers of John the Baptist.
2. The controversy with the Jews.
3. The controversy with the Gnostics.

70 Why should John be in controversy with the Baptist?

To understand this controversy it is necessary to look briefly into the work of John the Baptist. In the Synoptics the great prophet of the desert is represented as a powerful preacher of righteousness who headed a numerous party. His sermons were practical, down to earth, and highly ethical and social in their import. In the Fourth Gospel he is represented as the herald of Jesus who steps out of the way when Jesus arrives.

The historical facts are, however, that the Johnite movement was a considerable problem to the church authorities, that the followers of the Baptist believed he was the Messiah, and that his work went on for many years after his death. The Fourth

Gospel indicates that the relative importance of Jesus and John was still a subject of debate almost a hundred years after the death of Jesus. When Paul arrived in Ephesus he found a militant group of Johnites organized there (Acts 18:25; 19:3-4). From writings of some of the early Church Fathers, we learn that not only was there a Johnite party in Ephesus long after the writing of the Fourth Gospel but they were still in conflict with the Christian Church.

71 How did John deal with the Baptist question?

It is very evident that he held John the Baptist in high respect, both on his own account and because of the favor he enjoyed at Jesus' hands. But because of his firm belief that Jesus was the Son of God he could not accord to the Baptist an equal status. He therefore presented him as the herald of Jesus whose business it was to announce his coming and then make way for him. In doing so he represents the Baptist as having testified to Jesus' divinity (1:19-51), thus claiming the Johnite movement for Christianity. It is extremely interesting to note that whereas the Synoptics tell in some detail about Jesus' baptism at the hands of John, as though he might have been one of John's disciples for a time, the Fourth Gospel makes no mention of any discipleship but represents the Baptist as paying tribute to Jesus. The entire treatment of the question leaves one with the feeling that John is trying to win the Johnites over to the Church at the same time that he is relegating the Baptist to a subordinate position.

72 How did John deal with the problem of the Jews?

We must forget that the early Church was beset with enemies without and within. The rapid spread of the faith can easily deceive us into thinking that it was thrust out into a world that was eagerly awaiting it, but such was not the case. It was necessary to contend strenuously for every gain that was made, and the Gospel of John represents a part of the struggle.

In Jesus' day Jews offered opposition to him and to his teachings, but that opposition centered about two major points—the ceremonial Law and the messianic hope. His opponents were the doctors of the Law—Pharisees, scribes, and legal experts. The criticisms they offered were all of a kind—he did not keep the Law.

In John's day the whole situation was changed. The Temple

was destroyed, and it was no longer possible for the Jews to insist upon a strict observance of the ceremonial laws. The Temple tribute was no longer collected. But Jews still offered violent opposition to the Christian movement. Now, however, they were no longer described as Pharisees, Sadducees, scribes, etc., but simply as "Jews"; and the Fourth Gospel is replete with references to them as the enemies of the faith.

73 What is the explanation?

Judaism and Christianity, as the two great ethical religions of the world, were face to face as implacable rivals. To the devout Jew the thought of more than one God was revolting in the extreme. He was willing to grant that God was preparing for the coming of a Messiah who should re-establish the Jews as a world power, but he could not think of such a Messiah as being also a God on a parity with Jehovah, the God of Israel.

John, on the other hand, saw in Jesus the incarnation of God (the Logos) who fulfilled the messianic hopes of the Jews, and he undertook to answer the objections they offered. In answer to their argument that no Messiah could be expected to come from Nazareth, John shows that that belief is no better than a trivial prejudice (1:46; 7:52). In answer to the charge that Jesus had died the death of a felon, he recites Pilate's declaration that he was no criminal (19:4). Judas' betrayal, the failure of Jesus' public ministry, and his lack of professional schooling in the Law (13:27; 6:64; 13:11; 7:15) are all explained. His death is portrayed as a self-determined act designed as a voluntary doing of God's will. The student who reads the Gospel carefully will find many evidences of this controversy between the Christians and the Jews in the arguments John puts forward. He even charges the Jews with no longer being Jews (see Question 10).

74 How could that be?

It was a cardinal belief among the Jews that God had entered into a covenant with the nation. As long as they remained true to him, he would continue to be their God. But John believed that the Jews, in rejecting Jesus, had forfeited their right to be called Jews—they had repudiated their part of the covenant. The book of Revelation called some of them "a synagogue of Satan" (Revelation 2:9), and John countered their attack on the

Church by saying that they had alienated themselves from God by their rejection of Jesus (8:39, 44), and were no longer really Jews. The spiritual heritage of the nation, he believed, had passed over to the Christian Church, which was now the true Israel.

75 What about the controversy with the Gnostics?

Almost from the beginning the Church had been torn by controversy. Back in the early years of Paul's ministry the source of contention had been the question of "keeping the law." Then came various questions of doctrine and procedure. In John's day the Gnostic faith, with which we first became acquainted in Paul's letter to the Colossians, had moved out into the center of the stage.

It was one of the contentions of Gnosticism that Jesus did not actually come in the flesh, and that his death was an illusion. The Gnostics even cultivated one legend to the effect that Simon of Cyrene died in Jesus' stead. In contrast, then, John tells about the print of the nails, the spear wound, the cries of thirst, Jesus' weariness, and says that Jesus "went out, bearing his own cross," without even mentioning Simon of Cyrene.

He omits all references to angels or evil spirits, which might seem to support the Gnostic theory of many spirits. Scholars expert in this field find other evidences of John's controversy with the heretics, in which the Fourth Gospel takes the position that Jesus is the supreme revelation and incarnation of God, beside whom there is no other.

76 What was the purpose of all this controversy?

The evidence all points to the belief that the author of the Fourth Gospel was a Jew, familiar with Jewish religious traditions and practices, who had been converted to Christianity. As a spokesman for the faith (self-appointed, probably) he had set himself to the task of interpreting Jesus to the learned and intellectual Greeks in an effort to persaude them to make him their Lord and Saviour. In doing so he must, of course, meet the objections that were current at the time.

First of all he had to make plain the difference between Christianity and the Johnite movement. Then he had to explain why the Jews had repudiated Jesus, their Messiah. Finally he had to shake the Christian faith loose from the parasitic heresies. It was just here that he revealed what may have been his greatest skill.

77 Was he well prepared for this great task?

Knowing nothing of his scholastic training, we can only judge by his book. He lived in a city that was exposed to the winds of doctrine that came in from all over the world, and it is apparent that his mind had been well seasoned by contact with the Greek mind of his day. The Gospel he gave us is, probably, the most profound book in all the New Testament, but to sense its deeper meanings we must be ready to appreciate its use of a Greek philosophic vocabulary.

78 What need had John of a Greek vocabulary?

The average Gentile knew little about the Hebrew Scriptures, religious traditions or vocabulary. If Christianity was to thrive in the Gentile world, it had to be transplanted from its Jewish soil and heritage into the new Gentile environment. The Jewish wing of the Church had disappeared, and the whole future of the movement lay with the Gentiles. The faith, therefore, had to be made plain to Gentiles. This called for a considerable break.

79 What was the nature of that break?

The Scriptures to which the Christians referred for their proofs were, for the most part, unknown to the Greeks. The Jewish hope of a Messiah, for instance, stirred little enthusiasm in the heart of a Gentile. Why should a Greek hope for the coming of one who was to set up a Jewish kingdom? One of Paul's great arguments was that the Christian was liberated from the Jewish ceremonial Law, but the Greek had never been under it and needed no such liberation. The conflict between the Jewish and the Christian point of view could have afforded the average Gentile no more than a passing interest. Stephen's speech or Paul's defense before Agrippa must have struck the learned Greek as "much ado about nothing." When John wrote his Gospel in the city of Ephesus about A.D. 100, seventy-five years after the Resurrection and when Christianity was bidding for world support, the problem of faith in Jesus took on an entirely new aspect. To capture that world someone had to use Greek ideas, Greek words, and Greek thought forms and modes of expression. He had to meet the Greek mind in the field of speculative thought.

80 What did speculative thought have to do with it?

The Christian faith presented in Paul's letters and the Synoptics was *ethical* rather than *speculative*. It enjoined moral conduct but did not indulge in fine-spun theological abstractions. True, occasional passages on the Resurrection (I Corinthians 15:35-56) and immortality (II Corinthians 5:1-4) took on that form, but these were not characteristic.

The Greek, on the other hand, asked deep questions about God, ethics, and life. How can a man know God? What is the relation between the physical and the spiritual? How can the soul escape the body? These were the questions he asked and the meticulous care with which the Jew washed his body seemed ridiculous to him. If the Christian message ever captured the Greek, it must answer those questions.

81 How did John answer those questions?

It is very evident that John was a devout man who had had a transforming personal spiritual experience. He lived in a time when Christians could not talk about their experiences *with* Jesus, in the flesh, for he had been dead three quarters of a century. Their religion consisted of opinions *about* Jesus, or inner experiences in which the spirit of Jesus had entered their own lives. By this time the Church had begun to take Jesus' measure, John had asked the question, "What kind of person was this man?" and had found his answer; but to make that answer intelligible to the Greeks he had to use words with which Greeks were familiar. As one reads John's Gospel he has the feeling that the author had had an amazing personal experience by which a new quality of life had entered into him through his belief in Jesus. This had convinced him that Jesus was the actual Son of God. His Gospel represents his conclusions, now that he had time to think about his experience.

82 What about those Greek words?

There are three of which he makes a good deal—all words which had a peculiar and special meaning to the Greeks. If we

33

refer to a good concordance, we can make some extremely interesting comparisons, as indicated in the following table of the number of times these words occur in the four Gospels:

	Matthew	Mark	Luke	John
Light	7	0	5	21
Life	6	3	5	33
Believe	9	13	7	90

In the great majority of instances, when John uses any of these, they have for him a special meaning and a definite Greek connotation.

83 What did "light" mean as John used it?

Among the Greeks, and especially among the Gnostics, the word signified knowledge, particularly that knowledge which has to do with God and the spiritual life of man. Among the philosophers the words was used as a name for an actual presence, or active influence, at work in the world illuminating the minds of men. John used the word in that sense when he called Jesus "the light of the world" (8:12; 9:5). He was the incarnation of this "presence" or "active influence" to which the Greeks referred when they used the word. This, it will be noted, was entirely different from any meaning the Jews attached to the word. Only one skilled in Greek would have used it in such a way.

84 What did the word "life" mean?

Among the Greeks the word had two meanings—physical existence and something much more significant. The body, according to their thinking, imprisoned the spirit of man and prevented it from establishing contact with God on a purely spiritual basis. Humanity, because of its "fleshness," is shut away from the true life which is in God; and, try as we may, the gulf can never be bridged. Throughout one's whole existence the spirit is engaged in a struggle to free itself from its captivity. The great aim of existence is to achieve the life of the spirit.

John was conscious of a new life that had begun in him when the spirit of Jesus entered his spirit. This was a result of his faith in Christ. Christ possessed life, having received it from God, and was able to impart it to others. "In him was life" (1:4a) and "to all who received him . . . he gave power to become children of God" (1:12). The reason for Jesus' coming was that he might impart life more abundantly (10:10) to all who would accept it. When Jesus died he actually entered into a new life which enabled him to keep in touch with his followers and become in them a living presence. Anyone who will may enter into a union with this living Christ and thereby be allowed to enjoy a new quality of life. Thus, according to John, not only did Jesus' memory survive but also his personality and presence. He still lives, though in a higher degree of being, and is present with his followers.

85 What did John mean by "believe in him"?

Stated in its simplest terms, it meant to open our hearts to receive his spirit and obey his commands. The Christians were to take something of the attitude that was taken by the original disciples. They were to meditate upon his words, ponder over the meaning of his deeds, and seek by all the means at their command to put themselves into a state of mind and heart whereby his spirit might enter into theirs.

For centuries the Greeks had believed that divine powers entered into men under certain circumstances, causing them to utter sacred words or speak divine truths. Here and there shrines were to be found whereat, it was believed, the spirit of some god had entered into some man. Some of the words spoken by these inspired individuals were called oracles, and were held in high reverence. John's explanation, then, of the experience of a Christian who believed in Jesus and as a consequence received from him a new experience was readily understood by the Greeks who heard it from his lips. If they would open their hearts to Christ he would come in and impart an entirely new spirit, something they could not achieve by their own efforts.

86 Did John make special use of any other Greek word?

There is at least one more which we should examine with some care, for around it is draped one of the most important doctrines John preached. One cannot understand the Fourth Gospel if he has no understanding of John's use of the word "Logos."

87 What does "Logos" mean?

It is a Greek word which has been translated into the English as "Word," but really to understand it in the sense in which John uses it in the first eighteen verses of his book, we must make a brief study of the philosopher Philo.

88 Who was Philo?

In the city of Alexandria, Egypt, there were many Jews, and among them much culture and learning. The city boasted of one of the great universities of the time. Out of this cultured life there appeared a philosopher named Philo (20 B.C.?-A.D. 50?), who became world famous for his learning. He had been trained in the faith of the orthodox Jews and schooled according to the best Greek standards. As a devout Jew, he found it impossible to believe the universe was purely impersonal, and, as a learned Greek, he felt a lack in his Hebrew religion. In an effort to explain the universe in terms satisfactory to a believer in a personal God such as Yahweh, the God of the Jews, he developed the doctrine of "the Logos."

89 What was the doctrine of the Logos?

The Greeks believed the universe to be "reasonable," by which they meant about what the modern man means when he says it is "rational." They believed it to be subject to a reasonable explanation. Their word "logos" meant either "reason" (thought) or "word." Now Philo taught that there was a personal Creator back of the universe, out of whose person an "influence" had gone forth to order and rule the world. To this "influence" he gave the name "Logos." His Jewish training had taught him that there is but one God, and as a consequence he could not bring himself to think of the "Logos" in terms of a separate divine personality. But he had taught so effectively this doctrine of an "influence" emanating from God that learned Greeks everywhere were familiar with the meaning of the word, and used it generally, somewhat as we today speak of "evolution." In its simplest terms it meant "the creative and maintaining spirit of God which is active in the world."

90 Did Philo invent the doctrine of the Logos?

No. Various Greek philosophers—Heraclitus, Plato, the

Stoics—had speculated about the logos through a good many years. But very likely the author of the Fourth Gospel came to his conception by way of Philo's doctrine of the Logos.

91 How did John use the idea of the Logos?

He saw in the word and the doctrine exactly the thing he needed to explain Jesus to the learned Greeks of his day. First of all, he identified the Logos with God (1:1) and then proceeded to declare that Jesus was the Logos, as he appeared among men in the form of a man (1:14). In other words, the Logos of whom Philo had taught had actually assumed the form of a man for a brief space of time and had lived among men, had been seen and known of men, had been given a name, and had left a body of teachings by which men were to be guided. In the last words of his book John declared it to have been his purpose so to present the case of Jesus that men would believe he was truly the Logos and at the same time the Son of God.

Having identified Logos with God, John proceeded to explain Jesus in terms of the Greek interest in "life" (Question 84, "light" (Question 83), and "belief" or "truth" (Question 85). The supreme gift which men hoped to receive from God must come through him; he bestows upon men the power to become "children of God" (1:12)—another concept—as familiar to the Greeks as to the Hebrews. He was the source of life and light (1:4), having existed alongside of God from the beginning (1:30; 8:58; 17:5). "The words that I have spoken to you," says Jesus in John's Gospel, "are spirit and life" (6:63).

92 Where did John get this idea?

As has been said, Philo had made the idea familiar to well-educated and thoughtful Greeks everywhere. There were many such in Ephesus, and John could easily have absorbed the general idea from conversations with learned citizens, from listening to philosophical lectures delivered in the lecture halls of Ephesus by traveling teachers. It would have been difficult for a thoughtful man to have mingled with other thoughtful men in the city and to have escaped hearing the idea discussed. But the interesting thing to us is the way John appropriated the idea and worked it out.

In the first eighteen verses of his book he stated the doctrine in Christian terms, and asserted that Jesus was the Logos in the form of a man. Having thus connected Jesus with a popular Greek concept, he proceeded to describe Jesus, his work, his person, his divinity, as the Logos, in a way which he hoped would convince and convert the Greeks. Having identified Jesus with the Logos in his introduction, however, he proceeded to describe him without again mentioning the word "Logos." In doing so he used an intersting form of presentation, altogether different from anything else in the New Testament.

94 What was there about his presentation that made it peculiar?

In the Synoptics an event is described and the reader is allowed to make his own observations concerning its meaning. The authors thought of themselves as reporters rather than as theologians. John, on the other hand, felt himself under an additional obligation—a responsibility for explaining the inner spiritual significance of events. To him Jesus was a divine person doing a divine and supernatural work, and as such had to be explained. In the Gospels of Mark and Luke, as well as in the current traditions and popular stories with which he was well familiar, he found an abundance of material which described our Lord and his life, and from this mass he selected certain typical events and situations which explained Jesus and exhibited his divinity. He therefore chose his incidents because of their value as evidence, recited them, and then explained their significance. Thus we find in John many instances of the story of an occurrence followed by a lengthy explanation of its inner spiritual meaning.

95 Can you cite some of these?

There is the conversation of Jesus with Nicodemus, for instance. It is found only in John's Gospel (3:1-21). It is full of allusions to Greek philosophical concepts and uses some Greek terms. The first twelve verses describe the visit, and the next nine set forth its inner message. In the next chapter the story of the woman at the well is told in the same way. First comes the report of the incident (4:7-19) and then the interpretation

(4:20-24). Again in the sixth chapter this form of argument appears several times (6:26-27, 29, 32-40, 44-51, 53-58, 62-63). As we read these stories with their interpretations, we finally become aware of the fact that John is using a device that calls for some explanation.

96 What kind of literary device did John use?

Several centuries before John's day Plato wrote a series of dialogues in which he portrayed Socrates as the leading character. Events were chosen out of the life of the great Athenian, many of them entirely authentic, and combined with speeches which Plato composed and put upon Socrates' lips. All the speeches were true to the spirit of Socrates and probably represented his mind with considerable accuracy. But no one who is familiar with Plato's dialogues has ever been deceived into thinking that Socrates delivered those speeches exactly as Plato wrote them.

In some such fashion John wrote the Fourth Gospel. He was steeped in the teachings of Jesus, familiar with the significant events in his life, and above all deeply affected by his own personal experience with the living spirit of Jesus. The Synoptics had reported his life, his teachings, and his activities. John now undertook to interpret all that everyone might know *what* Jesus was, the Synoptics having told *who* he was.

97 Had not Paul done this already?

Paul was the first Christian to write a complete book for the New Testament. He lived almost within the sound of Jesus' voice, and professed to have seen Jesus in the spirit (II Corinthians 12:2-4). He may even have believed that he had actually seen him in the flesh (II Corinthians 5:16), but in his preaching and writing he attached little importance to the historical Jesus. Aside from his death and resurrection and a single scene from the last supper, Paul made no reference of any sort to anything that ever happened to Jesus while he preached in Galilee and Judea. He was content to emphasize the necessity of faith in Jesus Christ, the risen and glorified Lord who sat at the right hand of God.

Just as Paul discarded the demands of the Jewish Law as a part of the Christian faith, John discarded the idea of a political Messiah which had always been so conspicuous in the thinking

39

of the Jews. To him the earthly life of Jesus was of spiritual significance because it was the form in which God had revealed himself in the flesh. He was interested in the Master's death and resurrection, of course, and told the story (chapters 18-20) much as it was told in the Synoptic Gospels. The resurrection had gone far to convince him of Jesus' divinity, but he also saw that there was much more in the life of Jesus while he was busy in Galilee than was realized by those who saw him alive and heard him preach (16:12-14). It was this "much more" which John attempted to set forth in his Gospel and which represents his unique contribution to Christian thinking. It also explains some of the peculiarities of his style.

98 Was there anything peculiar about John's style?

The casual reader will probably be impressed with a peculiar sentence form in John's Gospel in which the word "and" is used with great frequency (9:6-7, 11). Papyri fragments which have come down to us from that period show that it was a popular form in common use in that day among the plain people.

A second peculiarity is his use of questions and answers, as in the story of Nicodemus (3:1-21), the woman at the well (4:7-26), the lame man who was healed (5:5-9), and others. A comparison of these accounts with the Synoptics brings out the fact that this style is John's own, and through it he introduces statements which do not appear anywhere else in the Gospels.

One of the chief problems of the Fourth Gospel, however, is his use of what is known as the "I" style, and this calls for some special investigation.

99 What is the "I" style in John?

There is a marked use of the pronoun "I" in the book. Read John 10:7-18 and notice the number of times it appears. Comparing the Fourth Gospel with other religious writings of about A.D. 100 we make the interesting discovery that such usage was common in that day, the authors very frequently using the pronoun "I" where a modern author would use the pronoun "he." Now read the John passages again, inserting "he" for "I," and immediately we discover that John in them is confessing his own faith.

100 What does this mean?

John was, as has been said, a Christian preacher of Ephesus

who was trying to persuade the Ephesians that Jesus was the Son of God. He had become convinced of this through a profound spiritual experience of his own, and he believed that every Christian who has really established contact with Christ is like a branch which draws its life from the vine (15:1-7). Life is something Christ imparts to those who obey his commandments and commit their lives to him. In an effort to convey his convictions to his readers he composes long speeches, puts them on the lips of Jesus, and offers the whole to the public as a historical narrative.

101 Is this not taking great liberty with scripture?

Again it must be said that John had no thought that he was writing scripture. He was only attempting to write a convincing argument which would prove to the Greeks that Jesus was the divine Son of God. Just as a modern author feels justified in putting words on the lips of his characters, so John undertook to make Jesus speak for himself. And because he believed the speeches he composed were a true and faithful representation of Jesus' spirit and mind, he was perfectly honest in using the method he did.

102 How did John know Jesus' mind?

He had available to assist him (1) the Synoptic Gospels in which many of the precise sayings of Jesus were preserved, (2) the oral tradition current among the Christians in which many other sayings must have been preserved, and (3) possibly scattered written fragments of which we know nothing today but which were authentic and reliable. Then, above all, John had had his own spiritual experience through which he had discovered some things to be true. The accuracy with which John interpreted the mind of Jesus has been demonstrated down through the ages by those who have accepted his explanations, trusted his words, and found them true.

103 Does John differ from the Synoptics in his interpretation?

The reader must have been impressed by this time with the fact that the Fourth Gospel is very different from the Synoptics in many ways, but the differences can all be explained on the basis of the fact that John's interpretations represent the matured Christian thinking whereas the Synoptics represent the observations of those who were in immediate touch with Jesus. The Gospels of Matthew, Mark, and Luke are a record of the things Jesus said and did; the Fourth Gospel is a statement of what a profound Christian thinker thought about those things almost a hundred years afterward.

The Synoptics, for instance, have much to say about the Kingdom of God (sometimes called the "kingdom of heaven"), which was to be a new social order set up among men. John, on the other hand, had much to say about the divine nature of Jesus, and little or nothing about the Kingdom. He believed that Jesus imparted to his followers a new quality of life which he called "eternal life," and that they enjoyed it here and now. It was precisely at this point that he broke with an important Christian tradition.

104 With what Christian tradition did he break?

The doctrine of the second coming of Jesus. We have already discovered, in our study of Thessalonians, how much emphasis was laid on this hope by Paul. Then in Jude and II Peter we came across the matter again, as also in Hebrews and, to a lesser degree, in II Corinthians. From the very first there was a fixed belief among the Christians that Jesus was to return at an early date and complete his messianic work. This hope had sustained them under the word persecutions when their numbers were few and their cause despised. As time went on the hope dimmed because of the delay and a sense of deep discouragement overtook them. In John's day the courage of the Church in this matter was at a low ebb, and John had to face the problem and explain the delay.

105 What explanation did he offer?

He declared that the hope had not failed, but that it had been fulfilled. It had come to pass, he said, but people had missed it because it had not occurred as they had expected it. In his own experience he had felt an inflow of a new life upon his own soul, and this he declared was the inward presence of Christ himself (14:18 ff.). At his death Jesus had thrown off all limitations of time and space and had reasserted his spiritual nature—the nature he had laid aside when he "became flesh and dwelt among us." Now, in this new relationship, he stood ready to take up his residence within the hearts of the believers. Before his incarnation he had lived but had not been recognized by men. Now he could be apprehended by any believer, and where he was made welcome he would come in and make that heart his abiding place. "The Counselor," of whom the believer is conscious in moments of exalted spiritual experience, is none other than Jesus himself returned to have fellowship with his followers. Instead, therefore, of looking for a spectacular second coming attended by celestial fanfare, John declared that the promise "I will come to you" had been fulfilled.

106 Was this explanation accepted by the Church?

Not entirely or immediately. It is extremely interesting to discover that the Fourth Gospel had to win its way with the Church, and that it was opposed by at least a few in a vigorous fashion. There are writings of the ancient Church Fathers far down in the second century which indicate that the book was questioned very seriously. Some even declared that it was no "gospel" at all. But the good sense of the Church prevailed, and every New Testament the Church has ever had has included John's Gospel alongside the Synoptics.

107 What was the reason for the opposition?

The exact reasons are not clear, though two factors seem important: (1) there was some doubt about its having been written by an "apostle" (2) and there was some hesitancy about accepting all the implications of John's interpretation of Jesus.

108 Were those doubts reasonable?

The early Church fixed a rule to the effect that nothing should be included in the New Testament which did not have apostolic or Pauline authority, and that probably was a wise rule. But we know that some besides the apostles did have some important and valuable things to say about Jesus Christ and the Christian faith. Whatever the final decision may be about the authorship of John's Gospel, this will not alter the fact that down through the centuries it has been the most formative and influential of all the Gospels, and that more Christian doctrine has been quarried from its great passages than from any other book in the New Testament.

Mention has been made of the fact that it was opposed by some, but by A.D. 130 it had taken its place beside the other three Gospels, never to be displaced. During the centuries since that time its great doctrines of the Spirit of God, the incarnation, and the pre-existence of Christ, its solemn declaration that Jesus was the supreme revelation of God, and its adaptation of the Greek ideas of light, life, love, revelation, spiritual freedom, etc., have made it the keystone of the New Testament arch which declares the deity of Jesus. It can be said that if we had no other Gospel than John's, we still would have had a Christian Church preaching God incarnate in Jesus Christ. It is not unfair to the Synoptics to say that the Gospel of John is the only one of the Four Gospels upon which the entire structure of Christianity could have been raised. It could have sustained the Christian Church if it had stood alone.

110 How is the Fourth Gospel related to the Epistles of John?

There are three small books in the New Testament which bear the name of John. Numerous problems of authorship emerge as we study them carefully, but there is pretty general agreement among the scholars that they must have been written by the same person, and there is no good reason to believe that he was any other than the author of the Fourth Gospel. Among the scholars they are called "general epistles."

111 What does "general epistle" mean?

The name is applied to them because they are supposed to have been addressed to the Church in general, though First John may have been intended for some specific group of Christians.

112 For whom was First John written?

No one knows precisely. It bears no address, and no individual or group of individuals is mentioned. Rather peculiarly, no proper names appear anywhere in the book except those of God, Christ, and Cain. If we knew for a certainty to whom it was originally addressed, we could clear up several allusions which are now almost meaningless.

113   When was the book written?

There is nothing in the epistle which answers this question, and it becomes necessary to follow somewhat the same process of investigation as in the case of the Fourth Gospel. We know it is quoted in Polycarp's epistle (*ca.* A.D. 117); the Christian principals are referred to as "the old commandment" (2:7), indicating a late date; there is no mention of any conflict between Christians and Jews inside the Church—which also suggests a late date, when the Church was entirely Gentile. On the basis of such facts it is widely agreed to date it about the same time as the Fourth Gospel (95-115).

114   What do we know about its authorship?

For almost every verse in the epistle there is something very similar to be found in the Fourth Gospel. The vocabularies are much the same, except for the fact that the Gospel uses the word "believe" and the epistle uses the word "know." The great thoughts of the Gospel are often even better expressed in the epistle—which might indicate that it was written later than the Gospel and represents John's thought even more matured. At last it all indicates a common authorship, and in the absence of any evidence to the contrary we are justified in assigning it to John the author of the Gospel.

115   Is it really a letter?

It has none of the characteristics of a letter, carrying neither an address, a salutation, nor a complimentary benediction. It is, rather, a little homily or preachment.

116   What is its purpose?

It aims to confirm the Christians in their faith. It does not pretend to tell them new truths, but it elaborates some of the old truths with which, as Christians, they were already familiar (2:7, 20; 4:16) and vouches for their trustworthiness (5:13). There is a special purpose, however, which it attempts to serve.

117   What is that special purpose?

It seems that some heresy had made its appearance among the Christians and that some of them had separated themselves from the Church and organized an independent group.

118 What was the nature of the heresy?

It is impossible to speak with complete accuracy in this matter, though it seems to have been a form of Gnosticism. This is likely, for the Gnostic cult was strong in Ephesus and the surrounding region. At any rate, the heresy denied that Jesus was actually a human being like other men (2:22; 5:5) and assumed that his death had no significance because he was incapable of dying (4:3; 5:6, 8), since he was essentially a spiritual being.

119 What effect was the heresy having upon the Church?

It seems that many of those who had broken away from the Church were the more intellectual—at least they pretended to greater intellectual interests. Perhaps today we would call them the "intelligentsia." At any rate, they professed to enjoy a higher type of spiritual experience than plain people, and the plain people in turn were a bit envious of their superior status.

120 Were the heretics really a higher type of Christian?

They were about the same type of person as those who today assume the superior attitude. Their doctrine made no place for sin, for they believed they had become so spiritual that they were beyond all possibility of sin. Therefore they asserted that they could do as they pleased and be subject to no moral law, for all such subjection belonged to the inferior level of life. They were proud, exclusive, and unloving, and John undertook to show the Christians that they were actually inferior. He laid down certain standard tests by which we may judge our spirituality.

121 What were the tests he imposed?

It is impossible to furnish any specific outline of the book of John for the reason that it follows no particular plan. It is discursive and almost conversational in style, but three ideas emerge, connected by the passage "By this we know" (2:3; 3:16, 19, 24; 4:2, 13; 5:2), which are the tests.

1. There is *the ethical test*. Christians are expected to measure

46

up to certain moral and ethical standards. If we live according to them, we give evidence of spiritual integrity (2:3ff).

2. There is the *question of belief*. If we believe and confess that "Jesus Christ has come in the flesh," the Spirit of God is active within us. Then we may be assured that we are spiritually minded and acceptable to God (4:2 ff.).

3. Finally, the test of *brotherly love*. John teaches that love is the nature of God and that those who possess love have shared in God's nature. By reverse logic, those who are possessed by God will exhibit that spirit of love as an inevitable consequence. As we love one another we exhibit the Spirit of God which is within us (4:20), and earn the right to be called "spiritual."

 What is the difference between the epistle and the Gospel?

The Gospel is a book of devotion. It contains no great ethic such as is found in the Sermon on the Mount in Matthew. Rather, its concern is to explain the implications of the divine nature and work of Jesus. Therefore the ethical side of Jesus' message gets comparatively little attention. The epistle, on the other hand, is intensely practical. The inward experience is attested by practical activity. There is some of the practical quality of James in it (James 1:22). Deep spirituality is evidenced by our willingness to accept in good faith the day-by-day responsibilities laid upon us by life itself. John lived when wild speculations were distracting the loyalties of Christians, and when fantastic rules of conduct were being urged upon the faithful, obedience to which was called "spirituality." The epistle is an effort to call the Church back to its primitive moral sense.

123 How does the author call the Church back?

The heretics had questioned the validity of the ancient moral restrictions and principles of the Church, claiming to be of such spirituality that they lived beyond them. John comes to the defense of the ancient standards, which he calls the "old commandment" (2:7 and 5:2-3), and declares that they have been fully attested by time and experience. In this fifth chapter we come upon an interesting fact.

I John 5:8 refers to the "three witnesses, the Spirit, the water, and the blood." "Water" and "blood" probably refer to the sacraments (baptism and Holy Communion). But in the King James Version the preceding verse (5:7) mentions three others that bear witness in heaven. Now it happens that this verse is found in no manuscript that is older than the fifth century, and can be proved to have been inserted hundreds of years after the original was written for the purpose of strengthening the doctrine of the trinity. In all good modern versions the verse is eliminated as spurious, though it continues to appear in the King James Version.

125 Is this the only spurious passage in the epistle?

It is the only doubtful one in the epistle, but there is one in the Gospel which has a curious status.

126 What is the doubtful passage in the Gospel?

It is the story of the woman taken in adultery (John 8:1-11). A study of the oldest manuscripts reveals the fact that it does not appear in any of them, though we have no knowledge of just when it was inserted in the Gospel. It does, however, bear all the earmarks of being an authentic story and is accepted as being a part of the genuine memories of Jesus, though by what route or process it was saved and incorporated into John's Gospel we do not know.

127 What is the great message of First John?

It was the basic belief of John that the message of the Christian faith is vouched for by the deepest spiritual instincts of the human soul. The divine in man responds to the divine in God as the flower turns toward the sun (4:19). The epistle contains little that can be called doctrine; it is content to take its stand with love, goodness, and fellowship with God. These need no authentication: they prove themselves.

128 What is the heresy which the epistle combats?

Among the theologians it is called Docetism, and those who went off after it are called Docetists.

129 What does Docetism mean?

Among the Greeks there was a belief that all physical things were essentially evil and opposed to goodness. It was further believed that a good God would not permit himself to come in contact with anything so evil as a physical man, for this would expose him to the evil of material things. Some Greeks who wanted to accept the Christian faith tried to reconcile the idea of "the word made flesh" with this Greek doctrine of the evil nature of the physical man, and found it impossible. To get around the difficulty some declared that Jesus' divine nature descended upon him at the time of his baptism and left him just before his death on the cross. They also claimed that his physical body was not real, but some kind of an apparition. This meant, then, that his sufferings were not real but only seemed to be sufferings. The Docetists were "seemists."

130 How serious was the heresy?

There was a very real danger that the Jesus who died upon the cross would be divorced from the Jesus who returned to the souls of men and made their hearts his abiding places. This same danger is recognized in the Gospel of John, and the author kept reminding his readers at all times that the risen Christ who held communion with them was also the earthly Jesus who had lived and labored among men. The speculations of the Greeks threatened to carry the whole Christian movement off into the clouds, and the Epistle of John was an effort to hold it down to earth and keep it fixed to a practical and ethical basis.

131 Does this heresy also appear in the Gospel of John?

Not by name, but as we study the Gospel we discover that it was in the background of John's mind as he wrote.

132 How does the Fourth Gospel deal with the subject?

The basic idea of the Docetist heresy was this "seeming" aspect of the life of Jesus. The Docetists were willing to concede that Jesus had "seemed" to be crucified, buried, and tormented. If John were to meet the heretics in any effective way, he was under the necessity of affirming the complete and real humanity of Jesus. Instead of composing an abstract argument which

49

would prove the humanity of the Master, he chose a series of events out of Jesus' life which must have been quite familiar to his readers, and by linking these with the assertion that "the Word became flesh," he made his case.

133 To what use was the First Epistle of John put?

It was probably put into the hands of evangelists who moved about from church to church. Preachers like Demetrius (III John 12) who went about Asia teaching and exhorting carried the letter with them and instructed the Christians concerning the basic beliefs of the faith.

134 Were any other books written on this same subject?

Two other epistles in the New Testament are also ascribed to John and deal with the question of true and false teachers, though we cannot be sure that the same heresy is involved. In them we have very illuminating documents in spite of the fact that they are very brief little tracts.

135 Does their brevity have any special significance?

Both seem to have been personal notes and are almost exactly the same length. This is explained when we notice that they are just long enough to fill a single page of papyrus, exactly what we would expect a personal letter to be.

136 To whom were they written?

Second John is addressed to "the elect lady and her children," a phrase interpreted by some scholars as meaning "the Church in general and its membership." This, however, is disputed; for it seems more probable that a particular church is meant. We can be content to say that the letter is addressed to Christians whose identity is unknown but whose problem is reasonably well understood. Third John is addressed to "the beloved Gaius," who seems to have been one of the Christian leaders of a congregation.

137 By whom were they written?

The writer in each case is content to call himself simply "the elder," but it is very evident that he is a church official of considerable authority. It is with his approval that certain missionaries have gone throughout Asia preaching the gospel. There is no way of identifying the author except on the basis of the internal evidence of the books themselves, and such evidence all points to the author of the Fourth Gospel as being also the author of Second and Third John. If this conclusion is correct, we have four books from the one writer—the Fourth Gospel and the three epistles of John. The evidence that all were written by the same individual, together with the use of the name "the elder" in the epistles, strengthens the belief that "John the Elder" (or "presbyter") was the author of the Gospel, but it does not prove the case. It should be said, of course, that "elder" in this case does not mean "older" but is the title assigned to an officer of the Church.

138 What is the internal evidence as to authorship?

There are similarities between the two books which mark them almost certainly as coming from the same author, and also indicate that the author of the Fourth Gospel is the author of the epistles. III John 13-14, for instance, is almost identical with II John 12-13. Second John is full of phrases and even sentences which are to be found in Third John. Either one is copied in large part from the other or the same author wrote them originally.

139 For what purpose were these two John letters written?

Both of them deal with the question of preachers. As we learned in an earlier study in this series, the first years of the Christian movement saw men going about preaching in the name of Christ with no other credentials than their own interest and decision. Any man who could get an audience might preach. But as the heretical sects began to multiply, this system of "picking preachers" exposed the Church to serious dangers. Innocent congregations, unaware of the heretical tendencies of itinerant missionaries, were led astray by preachers with convincing manners and high-sounding words. We have seen how some great lover of the Church wrote words of warning to Timothy and Titus on this subject, and Second and Third John were written for the same general purpose.

140   What was the specific case of Second John?

The letter seems to be addressed to some church under the title "the elect lady" and concerns itself with the case of some missionaries who propose to visit it. John is much disturbed over the matter because they are teachers of false doctrine. It appears that they called themselves "progressive" (v. 9), but we have no exact knowledge as to exactly what their "advanced thinking" may have included. We do know, however, that the author warns the church very earnestly and insists that the simple truths which they have been taught are quite sufficient. His letter closes with strict orders that the "progressives" are not to be permitted to preach to the church. What authority he may have had for issuing such an order we do not know, nor do we know whether his instructions were carried out. All we have in the case is his letter of instructions.

141   What is the specific case in Third John?

In this case the situation is exactly the opposite. The letter is addressed to Gaius, evidently a local leader of the church, and charges him with the responsibility of opening the doors of the church to certain missionaries whom the elder is sending to them. From the letter we gather the impression that Gaius is the leader of a party that is friendly to the elder, and that the opposition is led by one Diotrephes, who had assumed the right to dictate the policy of the local congregation and had even expelled some who did not agree with him (v. 10). In this episode we get a glimpse of the developing church which is of very great interest and significance.

142   What does that glimpse reveal?

For many years the local churches were dependent for their preaching upon traveling missionaries. They were in much the same position as the frontier churches in the American wilderness shortly after the Revolutionary War. The vast multitudes of Christians were new to the faith and unprepared to instruct their fellows. In time, however, the local congregations grew in strength and began to assert their own powers. Paul's letters, the four Gospels, and other Christian writings circulated and instructed the people. People grew old and died, having lived all their lives in the faith. Famous preachers attracted little groups of students and small theological schools grew up around a few of the masters. Thus with the passing of the years the local congregations attained sufficient knowledge of the basic doctrines to be able to manage their own affairs, no longer dependent upon the traveling preachers. Second and Third John were written during the transition period and reveal two entirely different situations. In one case (II John) a church has to be warned against opening its doors to dangerous teachers, and in the other case (III John) one has to be ordered to receive certain preachers with courtesy and affection. The day is not far away when the whole Christian movement will have to take notice of the situation and make some provision for a system which will staff the churches with responsible pastors, satisfactory to the local congregations and also to the worldwide Church.

143 Did the same John write all the John books?

We are on reasonably safe ground in assuming that the same author wrote the Fourth Gospel and the three epistles, but we are not sure *which John* it may have been. In the case of the fifth "John book," however, we find ourselves dealing with an entirely different problem.

144 What is the fifth John book?

It is known as Revelation and is, in many respects, the most disputed and difficult book in the New Testament.

145 What makes it so difficult?

It is written in a literary style which has no modern counterpart. Readers who have had no experience with the style and who know nothing about the author's original purpose in writing, find it very confusing and, at times, altogether unintelligible.

146 What is its literary style?

Among Bible students it is called "apocalyptic literature." This was a peculiar form of expression which appeared among several peoples of the ancient East through a period of two or three centuries but has since passed completely out of use. It reached its finest flowering in the book of Revelation. One such book—Daniel—is found in the Old Testament. Jewish writers began composing in this style about the beginning of the second century B.C. and continued using it until late in the second century of the Christian era.

147 What was peculiar about it?

We are all familiar with the use of fiction; an author creates a story as a means of conveying ideas. We are also familiar with the literary device known as an "open letter," in which the writer addresses some well-known person in an intimate style, explaining ideas with the expectation that the public, as well as the individual to whom it is addressed, will read it. Then there is the dialogue method, not so well known to us but common in the ancient world. The writer composed a conversation between some famous person and one or more companions, and by this means the opinions of the famous one were expressed and discussed. Plato's dialogues are excellent illustrations of this method. Apocalyptic writing was still another type of literary expression, but because it has passed out of use it is necessary to explain its method and material to the student of today.

The Greek word "apocalypse" means "revelation." Applied to literature, it means a written account of a revelation; and in the case of a religious writing it means a revelation concerning the end of an era, or the end of time. The Hebrew prophets very frankly informed their readers of their judgments, basing those jugments on facts well known to all. In some instances they declared that their judgments were based on wisdom which had been imparted to them by some divine process, but in other cases they relied upon the reasonableness of their judgments to carry conviction and persuade the readers. An apocalyptic writer, on the other hand, made the blunt assertion that he had received a revelation from God and that his wisdom was not his own. He seldom offered any explanation concerning the circumstances under which he had received the revelation, and in the case of Revelation we have no information whatever. It was sufficient for the purpose of the author to declare that he had come into possession of his knowledge directly from God. We have to take his word for it.

148 Why should such literature be hard to read?

In Daniel and Revelation large use has been made of imagery.

54

Some of the scenes are depicted in the most extravagant terms. The symbols and figures used were understood by those who first read the books, but somewhere along the line we have lost the key and many of them are quite meaningless to the modern reader. As the author of Revelation builds up scenes portraying beasts, horns, harlots, trumpets, and dragons, we become confused, for we do not know what those figures meant to the ancients for whom the book was written; yet all those things had a very definite meaning for the people to whom the book was addressed.

149 Did the ancients understand the book?

It is extremely important that we keep clearly in mind this simple fact—*the author of Revelation intended that the book should be read and understood by the Christians of his own time.* Otherwise there would have been no point in writing at all. He intended to make himself plain; he had no desire to confuse his readers. Therefore he selected a literary style and used material which would convey his ideas to them in a way that would make his meaning clear to them.

150 Why did he use these symbols?

In the first place, those symbols were well understood by the people to whom he wrote. They may have been unintelligible to the Romans, but not to the Christians. Because his book is definitely seditious it is very evident that the author used symbols to conceal his real meaning from the officials of the Roman Empire and at the same time make it plain to the Christians. It was a device aimed to protect both the author and his readers from Roman wrath.

151 Who wrote Revelation?

The book of Revelation is different from many other books of the New Testament in that the author names himself. On five different occasions he speaks of himself as a prophet (1:3; 19:10; 22:7, 9, 18), but we cannot get far beyond that point, for it has never been certainly determined *which John* was meant.

152 Were there Christian prophets?

According to the belief of the Jews, the spirit of prophecy was cut off from them following the day that Ezra proclaimed the Law as the final and authoritative word of God (ca. 400 B.C.). As the Christian movement got under way, however, individual Christians here and there professed to have word from God, and as a consequence there grew up a class of Christian preachers known as "prophets," though the office always remained a secondary one (I Corinthians 12:28). It was, however, well recognized as a legitimate Christian activity (Romans 12:6; I Corinthians 12:10; 13:8; I Timothy 4:14; Acts 2:18; 21:9; etc.). The author of Revelation seems to have been one such, and apparently he was so well known to the Church that he needed no other identification.

153 Who could he have been?

As we found when discussing the Fourth Gospel, there were several Johns, and there are at least four theories concerning the authorship of Revelation.
1. It was written by the Apostle John.
2. It was written by John the Elder.
3. It was written by someone, now nameless, who ascribed it to the Apostle John in the hope that his name would get a hearing for it.
4. It was written by a Christian preacher of Ephesus named John, well known to his generation, who is otherwise unknown to modern Christendom.

154 What are the reasons for thinking the Apostle wrote it?

Early Christian tradition credited him with the authorship of the book, and several early Church Fathers, beginning with Justin Martyr (ca. A.D. 140), refer to the book as having came from the hands of the Apostle.

155 What reason is there for doubting apostolic authorship?

The authority of the book would have been greatly strengthened if the author had stated frankly that he was the Apostle John, but this he did not do. Instead, he describes himself as a prophet—which sounds strange coming from one who could have claimed apostolic authority. Additional doubt is raised by the fact that though an impressive list of Church

56

Fathers support apostolic authorship, others deny it.

156 What about John the Elder and Revelation?

There is a marked difference between Revelation and the other John books in literary style and vocabulary. The same words are used in different senses; the author of the Gospel conceals his name, and the author of Revelation announces his boldly; the Greek style of the Gospel is smooth, and that of Revelation is labored. In many ways the Gospel and the Revelation are entirely different. It seems very difficult to believe that the same author could have written both.

157 Did someone ascribe it to John?

The book of Revelation seems to have been addressed to seven congregations of Christians to whom the author was well known, and any pretense would have been quickly detected (1:9).

158 What about the unknown preacher of Ephesus?

This theory is supported by many splendid scholars, but the case is not proved. It seems evident that the book was written by a Christian Jew who was thoroughly familiar with the Old Testament Scriptures, that he had lived and labored in Ephesus, and that he commanded wide respect among the Christians. Beyond that we know very little about him, and, since no great doctrine depends upon the question of his exact identity, we can leave the question and refer to him hereafter simply as John.

159 To whom was Revelation written?

In answering this question we are on solid ground, for the information is supplied in the book itself, at the very outset (1:4). It is addressed to the seven churches—Ephesus, Smyrna, Pergamum, Thyatira, Sardis, Philadelphis, Laodicea (1:11)—and since the number seven represented "completeness" to the Jewish and Christian mind of the time, it is probable that the message was intended for all Christians. Certainly the essential message of the book is for all time.

160 Is Revelation a letter to the Church?

It opens in that style, though after the first three chapters that form of address is not used. This indicates the necessity of studying the two sections of the book separately.

161 When was Revelation written?

The book was written for the purpose of encouraging Christians who were face to face with persecutions. By studying the history of the early Church and noting the trials through which it passed we are assisted considerably in fixing the date of the book's composition. In making such a study, however, it is necessary to make at least a brief excursion back into Roman history and inquire concerning the emperor Nero.

162 What did Nero have to do with Revelation?

Paul had believed the Roman government to be friendly to the Christians. More than once it had protected him against the Jews (Acts 21:31-34; 23:12-24; 27:42-43), and he urged the Christians to obey its laws (Romans 13:1-7). It came as a terrible shock, then, when the emperor in A.D. 64 accused the Christians of firing the city of Rome and loosed the wrath of the government against them. Nero's persecutions, however, were confined to the Christians of Rome and did not constitute a general attitude of the empire. Moreover, the Christians were not persecuted for their religious beliefs, but because they were charged with being criminals. The Neronian persecutions did, however, warn the Christians that the empire's friendship was not to be trusted, and at least a part of Luke's purpose seems to have been to allay the suspicions of the empire.

163 What did Luke have to do with it?

One has the feeling in reading the Gospel of Luke that the author is attempting to show that there is no basic controversy between the Christians and the empire, and that the empire has nothing to fear from the Church. In any cases in which the Roman officials have had a chance to investigate the Christians, they have been exonerated. He tells how Pilate undertook to release Jesus and says that neither Herod nor Pilate found any fault in him (Luke 23:14-16). He makes it very plain that the difficulty was not between Jesus and Rome but between the Jewish authorities and the Master. He also tells how the proconsul at Corinth would not even entertain a charge against

Paul (Acts 18:12-16), how both Agrippa and Festus were agreed that there was nothing against the Apostle, and that he might have been released except for the fact that he had appealed his case to Caesar (Acts 26:31-32), thus taking it out of their hands. This, and other evidence, indicates that Luke hoped to improve the relations between the Church and the Roman government. The persecutions under Domitian precipitated the crisis, however.

164 What is the story of the Domitian persecutions?

In the city of Pergamos there was a strong Christian church (Revelation 1:11; 2:12) and also a temple erected to the honor of Caesar Augustus (emperor 20 B.C.–A.D. 14) where tribute was offered and the emperor had been worshiped as a god. Augustus, apparently, had not taken the matter very seriously; but the cult of emperor worship, having started, gradually gained in favor until Domitian came to the throne in 81, and thereafter it became a fixed policy of Rome. In the new emperor the Christians had an entirely new type of individual to deal with. Morose, suspicious, vain, ruthless, utterly without mercy, half mad, his viciousness broke all bounds in A.D. 93, and a program of persecution was launched against the Christians which reached out to the last confines of the realm. He was an enemy of every Christian everywhere.

165 What was his grievance against the Christians?

It is not possible to explain the entire situation in the brief space we have at our disposal in this study, but at least one of the sources of trouble can be described. The law required that the emperor be called "Lord and God." To Christians this was blasphemy (13:11-13), and rather than obey they faced the possibility of death (2:13; 6:9; 13:15; 17:6; 18:20). The likeness of the emperor appeared on the coins of the realm, and this involved the Christians in difficulties in the market; a Domitian priesthood ferreted out cases of those who refused to pay tribute to Caesar and reported them as disloyal; legal documents had to be attested by an oath involving the emperor; any appearance in court had to be attended by a similar oath. The Christian with a sensitive conscience was embarrassed in many ways every day.

166 What was the result?

It became dangerous to be known as a Christian. Whereas they had been persecuted by the Jews during the early years of the movement (2:9; 3:9), now they found themselves at war with the government. It was the Church versus the state. In refusing to pay the customary homage to Caesar they were cut off from many of the most enjoyable aspects of life. They were compelled to forfeit many social, political, and economic rights. Under such circumstances many surrendered, and the Christian leaders began to fear that the disaffections might wreck the movement. It was very clear to the thoughtful person that a real crisis had been reached.

167 Were any other religions involved?

Every other religion of the time, except Judaism, believed in and worshiped many gods. To add one more raised no moral issue in the minds of the pagans. Therefore the blow fell heaviest upon Christians and Jews.

168 Was the persecution widespread?

If affected Christians everywhere in the empire, of course, but it seems to have been most bitter in Asia Minor, for it was there that the Christian churches were strongest. And the case was not entirely unmixed; the empire did have some excuse.

169 How could such persecutions be excused?

Christian doctrines which seem innocent enough to us were viewed by the Roman government as being highly seditious, because they were not entirely understood. The Christians preached, for instance, that the empire was to end and that Christ would reign instead. Then in communities like Ephesus, where the Christian movement began to infringe upon the copper business and affect the sale of the images of Artemis (Acts 19:24-28), additional prejudices were aroused. In other cases, if disaster fell upon the land, it was easy to explain it by saying that the Christians had offended the pagan gods and precipitated the disaster.

170 What does Revelation have to do with the persecutions?

It was written for the purpose of encouraging the Christians to resist the empire and maintain their faith. It was a powerful appeal for spiritual loyalty, written in one of the most popular literary styles of the day and appealing to one of the most fixed convictions of the Christians. It was a ringing assurance to the Christians that their sufferings would soon end and that the Church would finally emerge victorious in its struggle against the state.

It is impossible to fix the exact date for the writing of the book (see Question 161), for the struggle does not seem yet to have reached its climax. But the author very evidently believes that great events are not far off; in his opening sentence he says that he is writing about "what must soon take place."

171 Where was Revelation written?

The Roman government used a desolate island called Patmos as a penal isle for political and religious offenders, and John declares that he saw visions while incarcerated there of the end that was to come (1:9). It does not follow, of course, that he wrote his visions down while on the island, though that could have happened. Because of the variety of visions reported in Revelation, and because of the extensive quotations from the Old Testament and other writings (nearly half of the book seems to have been borrowed from other literature), it is very likely that the period of composition extended over some time.

172 Why was John on Patmos?

He seems to have been one of the Christians who fell under the wrath of the empire and was imprisoned as a consequence (1:9b). What may have been the precise charge brought against him it is impossible to say. It is enough to know that he was one of the Christian sufferers.

173 What did John believe?

It is very evident that he believed a very terrible persecution was about to fall upon the Christians. The enemy (symbolized by a beast) would "make war on the saints" (13:7), and many would suffer for their faith (6:9-11; 7:9-17; 16:6; 17:6; 18:24). Antipas, the martyr (2:13), was only one of the first of a great multitude—"the first drop of the torrents that were to fall like a flood."

174 When was this to happen?

John fixes no exact date, but says distinctly that it was to come very soon (1:1). One gets the impression from reading his book that it was written during the lull that precedes a storm, and a careful study of all the historical evidence suggests that A.D. 95 could not be far wrong as an estimate. That would mean that John anticipated the terrible calamity to be impending about A.D. 100. If modern readers will fix some such date firmly in mind, they will find it very much easier to read the book and interpret its strange symbolism.

175 Why is that so important?

Many self-styled "students of prophecy" have undertaken to interpret the book in the light of modern events, saying that it is a prediction of the horrors of modern days of war. By ignoring the fact that John says the things he is predicting will come to pass "soon," and by reading modern events back into John's symbolism, they attempt to make him the predicter of today's history. But if language means anything, Revelation was written for the encouragement of Christians who lived about A.D. 100.

There is an additional reason for making so positive a statement. The Jews had many writings which predicted future events, and it was common among such that they were ordered sealed until a certain time. When the seals were broken and the predictions were found to be correct, the authors were justified and vindicated. The author of Daniel, for instance, had ordered that his writing be sealed (Daniel 12:9) as a test of the validity of his predictions. In the case of Revelation, however, the writing is not to be sealed but is to be read at once (22:10), for the events and circumstances of which it tells are *at hand*. This is the most convincing evidence that the book was written for its own times and is to be interpreted in the light of those times.

176 Why did John write his Revelation?

Like Paul, John seems to have exercised something of the office of a pastor. The burden of the churches lay heavy upon his heart. Throughout the entire book we feel the spirit of an anxious pastor, desperately concerned for the spiritual welfare of his flock. He may or may not have written his book on Patmos, but at last his visions began coming while there, and then when he wrote the record he clothed much of it in language designed to conceal its real meaning from the Roman authorities.

177 Why the necessity for secrecy?

His book was definitely seditious, and written for the purpose of encouraging the Christians to hold out against the empire. Therefore its encouragement to defiance was concealed under symbols and strange names which conveyed no meaning to Roman officers but were well understood by the Christians. For it John claimed the authority of Jesus Christ.

Whereas Paul had cautioned the Christians to live at peace with the empire (Romans 13:1-7), John in Revelation is defiant and rebellious. "Pay her back in her own coin, and give her double for what she has done," he says concerning the persecutions heaped upon the Christians. "In the cup she mixed for others, mix her a double draught. . . . Gloat over her, heaven! and all you people of God, apostles, and prophets, for God had avenged you upon her!" (Revelation 18:6, 20—Goodspeed.)

178 Does this appear in Revelation?

In the very first verse of his book John makes the claim that his writing is from Christ and that he is no more than the prophet to whom the message is revealed. We call it "the book of Revelation," but John called it "The Revelation of Jesus Christ." He deliberately claimed that Jesus Christ was the author.

179 What is significant in the name Jesus Christ?

It was John's solemn conviction that he was reporting a testimony conveyed to him by Jesus Christ. To John, as to other Jewish writers, God dwelt far off in unapproachable grandeur and conveyed his messages to men by means of some intermediary. Other apocalyptic writers reported that they had their messages from angels, but John declared that his had come to him through no other than Jesus Christ himself. The death and resurrection of Jesus might form the rock base of the gospel, but this book is a declaration that the risen Christ still speaks to his followers. For this reason he calls his message "Jesus Christ's testimony."

Because he believed that the vision which had been granted him was an essential part of the Christian gospel, he instructed his fellow Christians to read it aloud in the public assemblies of the congregations, where it was to have the authority of scripture (14:13; 19:9; 22:7, 14). Because the time was short there was none to be lost.

180 How could Jesus Christ be its author?

John did not mean to say that Jesus had dictated every sentence, word, and paragraph of the book. But he, John, had had the visions; they had been interpreted to him by Jesus; and in the book he was furnishing the Christians a true and accurate report thereof. In that sense he taught them that Jesus Christ was the author.

181 What about those visions?

Modern psychology admits that individuals here and there have strange and inexplicable experiences, but their value for the spiritually minded is usually open to serious question. In the case of the Hebrew prophets such experiences, when reported, had the effect of stimulating faith and courage. Moral issues were raised, consciences were sensitized, spiritual energy was generated, and action was stimulated. The value of Revelation arises from the fact that the same results are achieved even today when the book is read with genuine understanding. But it is impossible to explain all the circumstances surrounding the composition of the book or the experience of the visions. The symbols and highly imaginative style of the writing make it difficult reading for us until we have in some measure familiarized ourselves with its symbolism and underlying purpose.

182 How should apocalyptic literature be read?

It should be read just as any other literature is read—for the purpose of discovering, so far as possible, what the author was attempting to say to his original readers. While it is true that its basic message is timeless, it was written for a generation which lived at the close of the first century of the Christian era. It was meant to be understood by them, and we can never understand it if we do not know what it meant to them.

183 Was apocalyptic writing common in those days?

It was, both among the Christians and among the Jews. Though the Law was accepted among the Jews as the revelation of God's will, there were those devout individuals who believed they had messages for the nation which supplemented the Law. In the hope of getting a hearing for their messages, and knowing they would not be credited with having the gift of prophecy, they wrote their messages and frequently claimed the sponsorship of "famous names." In the course of the years a goodly number of such came into existence. Among them are the Apocalypse of Baruch, the Book of Enoch, the Assumption of Moses, and the Sibylline Oracles. Among the Christians it was not an uncommon experience for some "prophet" to arise in the midst of the meeting and report some message that had come to him from God.

184 What was the basic message of Revelation?

There was a belief which underlay all Christian preaching of the time to the effect that God was soon to intervene in human affairs because they had got completely out of hand, and that when he did so he was going to straighten them out, restore order, and establish his reign of righteousness among men. In other words, their hope was based on the belief that God was going to usher in a new age.

John believed that the Roman Empire had become so wicked, that it was so violently opposed to everything the Christian faith stood for, that it was so ruthless in its dealings with the Church, and that it was so certainly doomed that God was about to take a hand in the world's destiny and break up the empire and crush its power. When that day dawned, the Church would emerge triumphant. In an effort to prepare the Christians for that dreadful day which must soon come, and to strengthen their confidence that the victory of the Church was assured, John reported his visions in Revelation. Like other Christians he believed firmly that the Church was the heir to the promises of the Old Testament which had been made to Israel, so that he fills his book with allusions to the prophecies designed to show that they were to be fulfilled. If the student will consult with care a good commentary and read the references in the Revised Version, he will be surprised to discover how much of Revelation consists of material and ideas carried over from Old Testament sources.

The book is a ringing message to the Christians of A.D. 95, who suffered under the awful threats of Roman cruelties, that their sufferings will soon be over, for the triumph of Christ is near at hand. As John the Baptist proclaimed the nearness of the Kingdom of Heaven in anticipation of the coming of Christ, so the book of Revelation proclaims the coming of "the end," when the rule of Christ will be set up on earth and the Church of Christ will be the victor. There is something majestic in John's efforts to transmit to the Church his own unshakable convictions.

185 Was John correct in his predictions?

As a matter of fact, there is no exact record of persecutions falling upon the Church which can be definitely associated with the period in a way that makes it possible to say, "This was the fulfillment"; but we do know that the Church and the state were unalterably opposed to one another in principle—the Church relied upon moral idealism, and the state relied upon naked force. John saw that the empire, relying upon the emperor cult, was the mortal enemy of Christianity. Between the two there could be no compromise. The Church must stand out against it unflinchingly (13:10). Caesar, with all his pride, wealth, and glory of this world was pitted against the Church as it declared that *Jesus was Lord*. By resisting the state the Church set the pattern for Christian living for all time to come. That was the issue which John set before the Church in stark simplicity.

186 How do we proceed to study Revelation?

The book actually consists of two sections. The first consists of a prelude and a series of letters to the Christian churches of Asia Minor, in which seven congregations are chosen as typical. Then follows a series of visions, each of which is related in some way to the approaching "end." We shall first study the letters in some detail and then proceed to the visions.

187 What is the significance of the prelude?

The prelude consists of an announcement (1:1-3), the author's greetings (1:4-8), and a prologue (1:9-20). The announcement declares that the book contains the word of God which was given by Jesus Christ and was seen by John in a series of visions. Nothing could be more solemn than that opening declaration of authority followed by a three-fold blessing: (1) upon those who read it in the public services, (2) upon those who hear it read, and (3) upon those who heed its teachings. The author is attempting to make the most powerful appeal of which he is capable.

188 What is the meaning of the author's greetings?

In the next five verses the author commends himself to the seven churches. The words *"from him who is and who was and who is to come"* (1:4, 8) are a paraphrase of Exodus 3:14 which was in common use among the rabbis of the time, and are used here to direct the thought of the persecuted Church to God. Some authorities believe that the "seven spirits" refer to the Holy Spirit, the number seven being a symbol of perfection.

189 What is the meaning of the prologue?

The remainder of the first chapter is a description of the vision of Christ risen and glorified, who has commissioned John to speak to the churches (1:9-20). John says that he fell into a trance on the Lord's day (the first time in Christian literature that "the Lord's day" is named, and one reason for assigning the book to a late date) and heard wonderful things which he was commissioned to communicate to the Christians. Here we begin to find the symbolic expressions which are so characteristic of the entire book.

190 What do those symbolic expressions mean?

It is impossible to explain the symbolism of the entire book in the brief space we have available, but some comment on a few of the references which appear in the prologue will indicate the variety of the forms used throughout the writing. If we had a complete key which gave the meanings of all the symbols, it would greatly assist us in understanding the writing, but there is no such key. Many references in the later chapters are entirely vague, and may never be completely cleared up. The interested student will find it worth his while to study them with some care with the aid of a good commentary.

The *"golden lampstands"* (1:12) are a figure drawn from Exodus 25:31 and Zechariah 4:2, and refer to the churches, whose function it is to shed God's light upon the earth.

"One like a son of man" (1:13) recall Daniel 7:13 and is a messianic title. The *robe* that reaches down to his feet is a symbol of his dignity, and the *golden girdle* represents loyalty.

The *white hair* (1:14) is believed by some to refer to Christ's pre-existence and may have been borrowed from Daniel 7:9. The flaming *eyes* represent the condemnation of sin.

"Feet . . . like burnished bronze" (1:15) symbolize strength and stability and *"the sound of many waters"* (*see also* Ezekiel 43:2) may be a reference to the dashing of the sea on the rocky shore of Patmos.

The *"seven stars"* (1:16) and the *"two-edged sword"* (*see also* "The Word of God," 19:13-15*a*) represent the heavens that are subject to Christ and his judicial authority.

"The Living one" (1:18) was understood by the Christians to mean the risen Christ who had conquered death.

"The mystery of the seven stars" (1:20) means "the secret" of the stars and the candlesticks. The *angels of the churches* have been variously interpreted to mean messengers, bishops, and guardian angels, but the meaning seems to be *the essential spirits of the churches.*

Taken as a whole the meaning of the vision is that the risen Christ moves among the churches; they may be surrounded by paganism, but they are still in his care. The Lord who triumphed over death and the grave is the Lord of Life, the invisible and unconquerable master of human affairs. Therefore the Christians need not fear.

This brief excursion into the symbolism of the book suggests the complexity of the problem of the entire work, and indicates how completely the uninformed reader is dependent upon the work of the scholars in working out the meaning of the various symbols. It also suggests the extent to which the author has drawn upon the Old Testament prophecies (especially Ezekiel, Isaiah, Zechariah, Daniel) in phrasing his message.

191 Were the letters to the churches actual letters?

Chapters two and three consist of a series of seven letters, each one addressed to a different Asian church. They are all parts of one communication rather than a series of separate letters collected to form the book. They seem to have been chosen to represent types of congregations. Each church was expected to read the messages directed to the others, thus benefiting by the total message. The entire book of Revelation may have served the purpose of a modern circular letter intended for a number of readers.

192 What were the letters to the seven churches?

1. The letter to the church at Ephesus, 2:1-7.
2. The letter to the church at Smyrna, 2:8-11.
3. The letter to the church at Pergamum, 2:12-17.
4. The letter to the church at Thyatira, 2:18-29.
5. The letter to the church at Sardis, 3:1-6.
6. The letter to the church at Philadelphia, 3:7-13.
7. The letter to the church at Laodicea, 3:14-22.

193 What is the message to Ephesus?

Ephesus was the commercial and religious capital of Asia Minor (Acts 19:35) and a hotbed of superstition (Acts 19:19), its books on magic being notorious. After the destruction of Jerusalem (A.D. 70) it became headquarters of the Christian movement, and in John's day the church at Ephesus enjoyed a good reputation. It seems to have taken bold action against the heretics (2:6) and to have purged its ranks of false teachers (2:2), all of which was warmly praised. But the first glow of Christian experience had passed and the Ephesians had lost the fervor they had shown in the days of Paul (Acts 20:37); on account of this they are called to repentance (2:1-7).

194 What is the message to the church at Smyrna?

Smyrna was some fifty miles north of Ephesus and a close rival for all honors. There one might have seen a great temple erected to the honor of Tiberias Caesar. In the sixth century B.C. the city had been destroyed by the Lydians, and in the second century B.C. it had been rebuilt, so that the figure "who died and came to life" was especially appropriate and well understood. John is well aware of the suffering of the church, but as the pagan city rose again, so also will the church rise again. The hatred of the Jews was especially marked in Smyrna, and in A.D.

155 they even broke their Sabbath to burn Polycarp, the Christian bishop. The "synagogue of Satan" is an accusation against them and a declaration that they have forfeited the favor they might once have claimed at God's hands. The difficulties of the church at Smyrna are not yet at an end (2:9), but the faithful will eventually triumph and receive their reward (2:10).

195 What is the message to the church at Pergamum?

This city was fifty miles from Smyrna and fifteen miles inland. While it was inferior to Ephesus and Smyrna commercially, being less advantageously situated, it was superior to both in matters of politics and religion. In Pergamum the first temple to Caesar had been erected, and there the emperor worship had started—"where Satan's throne is" (2:13). The church at Pergamum had furnished at last one martyr—"Antipas my witness"—and had proved is faithfulness (2:13), but there was a heretical faction (2:14-15) who had compromised and tried to combine Christianity and the state religion. This could not be tolerated, and the church is called to repentance (2:16-17).

196 What is the message to the church at Thyatira?

Thyatira was about forty miles from Pergamum and was conspicuous for its trade guilds. The common meals of some of these guilds involved offering food to idols (as in the case of the bronze workers—2:18) and with this the Christians could have no part, yet it was impossible to be a bronze worker and hold aloof from their festivities, where heathen deities were honored and where the entertainment usually degenerated into an orgy. The church at Thyatira had taken a "liberal" position in the matter because of the influence of a woman who advocated "broadmindedness." She had called herself a "prophetess" (2:20) but she was a veritable "Jezebel." John saw the issue with complete clarity: a religion that was to redeem the world could not compromise. The woman is to be punished (2:22), and along with her those whom she has misled, as an example to the churches everywhere (2:23). Thereafter the faithful are exhorted to greater faithfulness (2:24-29).

197 What is the message to the church at Sardis?

The city of Sardis bore an evil reputation. Twice it had fallen before an enemy because of its own carelessness, and John's exhortation to the church there—"Awake"—could be well understood (3:2). The church was active and alert, as a matter of fact, but immorality had sapped its strength. John therefore warns the Christians sternly, but tempers his severity with assurances to the faithful (3:3-6).

198 **What is the message to the church at Philadelphia?**

The city of Philadelphia was some twenty-eight miles from Sardis. The life of the church at Philadelphia seems to have been of a high order, the Christians having endured their troubles with patience. It is assured that it will win many converts, especially among the Jews, and be protected by Christ during its dark hours (3:7-13). It is worth noting that long after all the other cities of the region had passed under Turkish domination, Philadelphia continued to maintain the faith and hold high the banner of Christianity.

199 **What is the message to Laodicea?**

The city of Laodicea was one of the richest communities in the entire province. It was the banking center for the district, supported a famous medical school, and was the seat of several great industries. All this had had the effect of dampening spiritual ardor, and the church there had become lukewarm and complacent. John hopes to awaken them to a realization of their condition, and promises them that Christ will yet bless them if they will repent (3:14-22).

200 **What is the essential message of these letters?**

By combining them in one composite we get a fairly accurate estimate of the spiritual state of the Christian movement as it faced the oncoming persecutions. It was making a heroic effort against tremendous odds, but it was also beset by certain strategic weaknesses. The spirit of compromise was strong within it, the influence of the surrounding paganism was deadly, there was a serious need for a standard doctrine among the Christians, and there was great danger that it would accommodate itself to the life and times amid which it lived. Clearly there was a desperate need for vigorous leadership inside the Church.

There is nothing in Revelation to indicate the reception his words may have had, for at the conclusion of the series of letters the book makes an abrupt shift. It had always been dangerous to be a Christian, and Christianity was not one of those religions which had a legal standing in the empire. But the time had come for the Church to face the issue with wide-open eyes, and John now proceeds to shout a clarion cry—"No surrender!"—and in the most dramatic writing of all the New Testament he undertakes to bolster up the courage of the Church. Instead of going down under the empire's persecution, the Christians must "overcome the world." In making his appeal John relies on a body of belief widely held among the Christians of the day.

202 Upon what conviction could John rely?

It was a characteristic apocalyptic teaching, popular in that generation, that evil must reach a climax before God would intervene and straighten affairs out. Jews as well as Christians held to this doctrine, and, proceeding on that assumption, John undertook to portray the wickedness and calamities of his time as though the peak had been reached and the intervention was imminent. To him, as to probably the great majority of the Christians, Caesar's demand that everyone should worship him as a god was the crowning infamy. They could not believe that God would be restrained longer. It is exactly at this point that one of the most interesting aspects of Revelation appears.

203 What is there especially interesting about that belief?

It was the belief of the plain people who made up the bulk of the Christian forces. They were not, probably, highly educated or especially intellectual. In our study of Thessalonians and Corinthians we learned that Paul made his most effective appeal to his fellow workers in the tent and sail shops. There is good historical evidence to show that early Christianity was a movement among the common people. It could hardly be expected that they should be conversant with the great and profound theological themes, and it was to them that Revelation made its most direct appeal. Without elaborating weighty theological doctrines, and by making an appeal to popular concepts widely accepted, John preached his basic and moving message—"Be strong! Fear not! You are to be overcomers!" In doing so he built his argument and arranged his book on the basis of three great ideas taken over from Jewish apocalyptic thought. The student will find it very helpful in trying to understand Revelation to keep always in mind the fact that John was appealing to beliefs commonly held by both Jews and Christians.

204 What was the first belief to which he appealed?

Basing their belief on various Old Testament prophecies deviously interpreted, the Jews believed that their Messiah would come to set up a new world order, judge the world, and establish righteousness. His coming, however, was to be preluded by a succession of disasters to which the name "messianic woes" had been given. Since the Christians owed their whole concept of the Messiah to the Jews, it was quite natural that they should take over this belief in the messianic woes as a part of the total teaching. We must remember that the Gentile Christians were dependent upon the Jews for their Scriptures and, in considerable part, for their interpretations of the Scriptures. Therefore this Jewish belief had also become a Christian belief of the times.

205 What was the second belief to which John appealed?

It was believed by the Jews, and in turn by the Christians, that before the Messiah appeared another figure—mysterious, half human and half demon, variously conceived and pictured—would appear upon the scene. This mystical figure was to be the incarnation of evil, and, as Jesus had represented God, it would represent Satan in a cataclysmic struggle for the possession of the earth. To this monstrous creature had been given the name "Antichrist," meaning "the opponent of God's anointed." The struggle between Messiah and Antichrist would mark the end of the age, and upon the result of the battle between them the destiny of the race would depend.

206 What was the third belief to which John appealed?

It was commonly believed among the Jews that there was a

counterpart of Jerusalem in heaven, built upon the grand scale, resplendent in glory and indescribably beautiful. The holy city of the Jews was held in greater affection by the race, probably, than was any other city of the world by any people. This belief in the heavenly Jerusalem had been heightened by the destruction of the earthly Jerusalem at the hands of the Romans, and in picturing the "new Jerusalem" of the Christian hope John was appealing to one of the most vivid doctrines of the day. With these three popular doctrines in the background of his mind, and in the background of the minds of the Christians to whom he was writing, John proceeded to set forth his visions in a majestic drama of three acts. The whole universe was his stage. The rolling thunders and heavenly hosts furnished his orchestras and choirs, Emperors, empires, the Church, and even God himself were the actors.

207 Are those three acts clearly marked in Revelation?

The first act might be designated "The Roll of Destiny," and is set forth in chapters 4-11.

The second act can be called "The War in Heaven," and is to be found in chapters 12:1-19:10.

The third act can be entitled "The New Jerusalem," and occurs in chapters 19:11-22:5.

208 Of what does the first act consist?

The prophet John writes that he was caught up into heaven, where he beheld God upon a throne surrounded by a host of angels: In God's hand there is a scroll where is inscribed the destiny of the world and the divine plan of redemption. It is so packed with destiny that it is written on both sides, but no one can read it because it is sealed with seven seals. Whenever anyone appears who can open it, the plan will begin to operate, but not until a Lamb arrives do the scroll and the seals yield. The Lamb, strangely enough, has been slain, and yet it is alive. As it opens the seals one by one, terrible sights appear—the angel of invasion, the angel of fear, the angel of famine, and the angel of death. When the fifth seal is broken the Christian martyrs under the altar cry out for relief. When the sixth seal is broken there is a terrific earthquake which shakes the whole universe. There-upon the martyrs praise God for their deliverance, for he wipes "every tear from their eyes."

At the very moment that the seventh seal is broken, seven angels appear with seven trumpets, which they blow in turn. With each blast some new disaster occurs. Just before the seventh blast there is a great earthquake. Then voices are heard in heaven shouting the good news that the mastery of the world has passed into the hands of Christ and that he is to reign forever and forever.

209 What is the meaning of the first act?

That Rome was the master of the earth was too evident to admit of question. No power on earth could challenge the empire. But in the Omnipotent Christ—the Lamb—it had more than its match (11:17), and he was very shortly to begin his reign and set up his new order among men. In the martyrs waiting under the altar and pleading for vengeance (6:9-11) John saw the hosts of those who had died for the faith. In their deliverance they were to have a vital part in the final outpouring of God's terrible wrath upon the empire that had hounded them to earth.

The entire act is a highly colored dramatization of the idea that all history has been planned by God and is under his control. The Christians need not fear, for he is the supreme and undisputed authority over the world's destiny, whose purposes cannot be shaken or turned aside. By the use of the number "seven" John kept the idea of perfection before his readers and in the center of the drama. It may be that disasters will shortly fall upon them, but they need not be terrified, for such are only temporary, and—what is more to the point—they are all under the control of God and are being used to work his will. Such a message must have been very reassuring to the Christians who awakened every morning to anticipate new terrors.

210 Of what does the second act consist?

The first act assured John, and the Christians, that Christ would win the victory over the forces of evil which were to war for the earth. But that was all in the future; the struggle had not taken place. The second act is a portrayal of the struggle, and the three chapters—twelve through fourteen—were probably meant to be the most significant in the book.

There is war on in heaven, the forces of God being led by the angel Michael. The conflict is only well begun when Satan is cast down to the earth, and there the old dragon vents his terrible wrath upon the Church. At this point the prophet sees an animal coming up out of the west out of the sea (Rome). From the land there comes another animal, which compels the people to worship the first animal (emperor worship). If any man has not upon him the beast's mark, he cannot buy, sell, or do business of any sort. But the prophet also sees the host of the ransomed saints and hears them singing a new song before the throne of God, and these have upon their foreheads the mark of the Lamb. In the midst of the song an angel appears, flying in mid-air and proclaiming the end of Rome. Thereupon seven bowls of wrath are poured out upon the earth, each one being the signal for a new disaster. As the seventh bowl is emptied, there is a wild shout, a terrific earthquake, and all is over. Rome falls.

As the scene closes an angel takes the prophet away to see the wreckage of the city. It is pictured as an adulterous woman, bejeweled and drunk with the blood of the martyrs, seated upon the seven hills (seven heads). There are also seven kings: five have fallen, one is reigning, and one is yet to come. Around the city as it burns are the kings, merchants, dealers, and navigators mourning the passing of the "harlot" who has made them rich, and from the throne of God comes a mighty chorus shouting the praises of God, who has triumphed. The Antichrist has been vanquished.

211 What is the meaning of the second act?

When the Emperor Nero killed himself in the midst of Rome, a legend began to spread throughout the empire to the effect that he had not really died, but that he had escaped to Parthia and would some day return to avenge himself on his rivals. As time went on and he did not appear, the legend took on more mystery, and there were those who believed he would come back in some spirit form. John, therefore, made use of this popular belief; but, instead of picturing him as coming back from Parthia, he spoke of his coming back from the "abyss" and making war by Satan's power on God's people.

The prophet does not name him by name, but uses a curious device known to all Christians of the time. To various letters of the alphabet the ancients ascribed certain mystical numbers, so that the numerical values of the letters in "Nero Caesar" added together totaled 666; and in John's reference (13:18) he made his meaning perfectly clear. The end of the age of evil is to come when the Christ of God has met this devil's messiah and destroyed him.

212 What does the third act portray?

Great heavenly hosts mounted on white chargers stream out to pay homage to their champion. The animal—Rome—and his vassal kings fall before the host, and Satan is hurled into the abyss. After a thousand years he is released to allow him to make one more futile effort against God's people, and when he fails there ensues the judgment. God is seated upon a great white throne, the dead are raised, the books are opened, and the new Jerusalem comes down from heaven to earth. Brightness, splendor, and light take the place of the horrors that have gone before. A river of life flows out from the throne to restore the earth, and the righteous people fill the city.

213 What is so difficult about all this?

The confusion into which readers of Revelation have fallen originates in two facts:

1. Because John's prophecy of the complete destruction of the Roman Empire proved to be mistaken, people have tried to read some still-in-the-future event into his book, with the result that it has become the happy hunting ground of the cultists. Self-styled "teachers of prophecy" have twisted its passages to make them predict modern events concerning which John had no knowledge and in which he had no interest.

2. Partly because of the necessity of protecting himself and his readers, and partly because symbolism was the customary mode of expression in apocalyptic writing, John filled his lines with fantastic imagery and mysterious figures altogether unfamiliar to the modern reader. Just because it is commonly known that all such had some hidden meaning, these same self-styled "teachers" have applied their own interpretations instead of discovering what the figures meant to the original readers, the result being distortions of John's message.

The remedy for all this is a good commentary prepared by a competent scholar who has investigated sufficiently to be able to define the meanings of the symbols in terms of their original connotation.

214   Was the book of Revelation a success?

Its value to the Christians of Asia Minor must have been very great, for they were badly in need of something to strengthen their courage, but as a matter of fact its ethical teaching is on a very much lower level than that of many other books of the New Testament. Some of its passages are bitter in the extreme, and the gruesome satisfaction that the prophet takes in the overthrow of Rome falls far short of Jesus' prayer of forgiveness upon the cross. As matters turned out, the persecutions did not develop to the extremes that John expected. Twenty years afterward Ignatius, one of the Church Fathers, found the congregations of Asia Minor strong and vigorous. Forty years later another great churchman, Justin by name, found the book of Revelation among the treasures of the Ephesian church, where it was prized as one of the most sacred possessions in the hands of the congregation, and where it was honored as a source of great spiritual inspiration.

215   How was it received by the Church in later years?

It is extremely interesting to note that, in spite of its explicit claim that it is scripture (22:18-19), it had a varied experience before it was finally accepted by the Church as such. Much violent controversy raged about it before it won its place in the New Testament canon. That section of the Church which followed the leadership of the church at Rome held it in high esteem almost from the beginning, but the Eastern church, strangely enough, was very much more reluctant. More evidence is found of its being used by the early Church, however, than is true in the case of any other New Testament book. Luther entertained serious doubts concerning it at first, though he finally printed it in his New Testament along with Hebrews, James, and Jude in an appendix. Zwingli, another one of the Reformers, did not accept it as scripture.

216   What is its religious value?

When we have drawn from Revelation its great stimulus to courage, there is not a great deal of religious value left. It makes nothing of the Christian virtues of humility, forgiveness, love for one's enemies, or any of the great deals of Jesus' teachings. Christianity, to the author of Revelation, meant loyalty to the